44 ON 44

44 ON 44

FORTY FOUR AFRICAN AMERICAN WRITERS ON THE ELECTION OF
BARACK OBAMA 44TH PRESIDENT OF THE UNITED STATES

Edited by

Lita Hooper   Sonia Sanchez   Michael Simanga

THIRD WORLD PRESS

Progressive Black Publishing Since 1967

Chicago

Third World Press
Publishers since 1967
Chicago

First Edition
Printed in the United States of America

Cover Design: Dana Gray
Cover art: Najee Dorsey www.artbynajee.com
Interior layout: Trish Frensky

Library of Congress Control Number: 2011921822

ISBN: 978-0-88378-317-7

16 15 14 13 12 11   6 5 4 3 2 1

ACKNOWLEDGMENTS

To all the people, unknown by most, some known by many, who fought this fight and gave their lives for generations so we could sing our songs and our voices would be heard. For those who voted early in the shadow of lynch mobs, to those who voted later in the footprints of our ancestors, we are thankful.

The editors would like to thank all the writers who graciously agreed to contribute to this anthology. We are especially grateful for the continued commitment of Haki Madhubuti and the staff of Third World Press to publish the work of African American writers. When this collection was originally conceived and Haki was asked if Third World Press would be interested, without hesitation he committed to publishing it.

We also appreciate the visual contributions of Najee Dorsey, whose painting captures the spirit of the election, and Dana Gray, who created the design of the book.

CONTENTS

Introduction: 44 on 44
Michael Simanga   xi

It's Been A Long Time Coming
Sonia Sanchez   3

Three for "O" in Light and Shadow
Askia M. Touré   4

Go! Be a Superhero
Renee Simms   9

Man, Roll the Window Down!
Patricia Smith   13

Brand New Morning
Randall Horton   15

Obama Shuffle
Frank X Walker   20

On the Road '08: A Speech for the Obama Campaign
Jasmine Guy   21

44, Sacred and Rising
Indigo Moor   24

What I Saw Shining on My Mother's Face
Ross Gay   25

Michelle Obama: Woman of Power
Pearl Cleage   27

Transcendence: Thoughts on Love and Race
Opal Moore   29

Barack Obama & the State of Black Women in Love
jessica Care moore   33

From 40 Acres to 8 Cents: A Married Couple's Ruminations
on the Symbolism of Barack Obama
Chuck D and Gaye Theresa Johnson   39

Imagine Obama Talking to a Fool
Amiri Baraka   47

november 4th: elegua in satin
LaTasha Diggs   49

Keep Living
Tina McElroy Ansa   51

Crossing Over: Invocation for the New Flag
Kelly Norman Ellis   55

Another Country
Natasha Tretheway   57

Bridge from MLK, Jr. to BHO, Jr.: Span of a Lifetime
Sala Udin   60

Passing the Baton: From King to President
Eugene B. Redmond   64

From King to Obama
Keith Gilyard   67

Receiving Line
Jericho Brown   72

President Obama and Organizing
Sababa Akili   73

Mrs. Pettawah's Journal Entry, January 20, 2009
Nagueyalti Warren   80

Contents

Litany at the Tomb of Frederick Douglass
Martin Espada   81

The Revolution is Being Televised!
Kevin Harewood   82

The Secret of His Success
Haki R. Madhubuti   86

Audacious Hope, Auspicious Signs:
Barack Obama and the Third Reconstruction
Shawn L. Williams   87

Inaugural
Sharan Strange   94

We Winter Still
Antoinette Brim   95

The Reckoning: A Prayer by the People
Malaika Adero   97

The Poem My Son Will Write One Day
Lita Hooper   100

On This Day, at This Moment—A Ghazal
Demetrice Anntía Worley   101

The Day the Earth Stood Still
E. Ethelbert Miller   103

Annual Martin Luther King Day Observation and March
Gloria House   104

New Day
Kwame Dawes   111

Malia at Lincoln's Desk
Tara Betts   116

Contents

White America's Trauma
Nathan McCall   117

Basketball Jones: Bofwana's Revenge
Tony Medina   125

The veil falls (Outside the womb)
Edward S. Spriggs   132

Educational Opportunity in the Age of Obama
Farai Chideya   133

Auto-correcting History
Parneshia Jones   137

First President and First Lady
Michael Simanga   139

Three Editorials (From Black Renaissance Noire)
Quincy Troupe   140

Contributors   151

Contents

INTRODUCTION
44 on 44

There is no way to quantify the impact of the Presidential campaign and election of Barack Hussein Obama. Not now. The depth of it can not be measured yet. The breadth of it can not be seen. We do know the ground shifted from the weight of those who walked a long walk over a long time to get to the polls and stood in long lines to vote for a new America, the one that belongs to all of its citizens.

In 2008, a social-political transformative opportunity arrived, seemingly out of nowhere, although we knew it had been on the way for generations. An African American man and woman, Barack and Michelle Obama, emerged right in the fold of a historic moment that gave rise to a movement that would bring significant change to this country and the world. It is similar to the Martin Luther King moment at the time of the Montgomery Bus Boycott, when the world sensed that a young, well-educated black man was stepping onto the world stage to play a central role in leading a historic change. Like the Civil Rights Movement and the other movements that emerged and converged in that period, in this time and with this movement there will be many battles, many victories, some defeats, but the United States has been changed forever.

While we can not yet quantify the impact of the 2008 election, we can continue the mass conversation, engage in the continued fight and document it with the voices of artists who are committed to etching not only the facts into stone, but also the soul of this time, the thought, the feeling, the flesh of it, the blood, the laughter, the anger, the fear, the enduring faith that, ultimately, the people make change. From that experience, we gather the bits and pieces of memory and collect our impressions, questions, expectations, disappointments and incremental progress. We amass the parts needed for future generations responsible for helping the world understand and remember why Obama's election was not only possible, but necessary. That understanding can only come if our stories are told, recorded and available. We have to leave our footprints in the concrete.

44 on 44 is a collection of writings designed to leave forensic evidence of what we witnessed and participated in. It contains work that was inspired during four periods: the Obama campaign through Election Day; the days leading up to the inauguration; Inauguration Day 2009; and the months after the Obama Presidency began. Purposely, this collection includes writers of varying levels of experience in writing and in life. Our intention was to record the story of this movement, told in 44 unique voices and in varying forms. The collection includes poetry, fiction, essays and speeches. This collection is a snapshot of the ways the movement to claim the presidency was felt and remembered. But we did not create *44 on 44* to be just a historical document. It is, most importantly, an invitation to remember that the movement to elect Barack Obama reaffirmed that we are the people and now is the time.

Michael Simanga

Introduction

44 ON 44

SONIA SANCHEZ

It's Been A Long Time Coming

On November 4, 2008, on that day when the earth tilted, I got up quite early to vote. However, the polling place had been changed so I had to search for my polling place. After I had voted, I walked to Brother Obama's Campaign office and reported to the workers that we needed to make signs to inform the people about this unannounced change. We made several signs with directions to the new polling place, taped them up and the people followed the signs where they would vote for this change coming at us all.

That night in Minneapolis, Minnesota, I watched the election of this black man coming out of the same cultural experience of family and neighbors become our first Black President and laughed and cried at the same time, and spoke to my father and said, "Dad, you said it would never happen in America. You said, not in your lifetime. But I had always told you that in my lifetime, from my Northern landscape, it would happen, because artists and professors and activists and mothers and fathers and human beings around the world had prepared our country and the world for this eventuality. And the earth is finally satisfied."

And I thought of another man, Brother Martin Luther King, and I remembered his eyes raining peace and social and racial and economic justice for us all. I remembered when Brother Martin spoke to Black people and opened his arms and heart he included all the people in his rainbow embrace. We knew that all people were his family. Just as President Barack Obama opens his arms, he includes the world. He says I have lived amongst Christians, Muslims, Buddhists—all types of people—his eyes and hands say I am all of you—just as you are all of me. Here is my hand. Let us lean into each other's breath and breathe as one.

Three for "O" in Light and Shadow

Young "O" stormed out of the Illinois plains,
a modern Nefertari striding by his side,
the salvation of a nation his quest-like goal,
as precious to his soul as his dusky bride...*

1. Sideways: Zen/Karma

Mostly, it seems, this life—this sacred, subtle,
ominous life—is itself a kind of karma.
Each of us human with a fixed number of breaths,
can, like Barack, attempt
to change our
zany World. Disciplined, serious,
dedicated, motivated adults—
like Barack and Michelle—moving
through karma—and that
will to move, that
motivation to speak,
reach out—to the human
family—a karmic response.

Myself these days, in serious
burn-out. Oh, the overall
response, warrior-instincts
are there, riding
the waves of outrage,
passion, social conscience. But,
somehow something
inside has pulled the plug
motivation-wise—and now,
I don't desire to move

that way anymore.
Now it's "another When,"
Sideways. Zen. "another
When." Balmy, blue skies,
breezes along familiar shores.
Whale-songs.
Rain, drizzle, puddles
among dazzling flowers.
The whole Mother
Earth motivation;
and young hearts,
minds, souls,
pure ones,
future lives
growing inside
our longing
for daybreak
beyond climactic
overkill. Youths are
the *actual* future
growing like tender,
green shoots and
tiny buds gaining
color, perfume,
among us.
And perhaps
we humans can
finally get it
right. Barack
and Michelle, in
cool, spring rain,
holding Sasha's and
Malia's hands.

2. Michelle/Glory:
   The Love-Fires Burning

Glow in your Nefertiti golden
dress, Michelle, my love, address
the Euro Ideal with soulful Chicago
Jazz, *Michelle Robinson of the Southside,*
Now Queen of America! First Lady of millions
liberated from Malcolm's
American Nightmare. The tall, amber
man, dignified beyond belief, strides
boldly beside you, while millions cheer,
thrilled and dazzled by the splendor
of their massive Direct Action, in bleak
neighborhoods, *Bushified* by poverty's talons.
Beautiful dreams by multi-millions
of democratic decency. Norman Rockwell,
maybe? But if millions dream it and live it,
then it grows from vision to national fact.
Right now, Comrades, don't remind me of
sinister politicos pulling strings—from Wall St.
to State St.; shadowy "operatives" bugging
phones, making hit-lists headed by a slim,
charismatic poet-orator with a mean,
left-hand jump-shot from mid-court.
Children's eyes sparkle from Watts, Harlem,
Chinatown, to the Barrios; they reflect
those of Sasha and Malia.
Tomorrow, the hard-core Race/Class analysis.
Tonight, this tall, voluptuous queen in
shimmering white gown, dancing with
Mister Wonderful, while Beyonce echoes
the soul vibrations of millions: *At Last!*

3. Jeremiah Wright: A Warning

In this great, virgin land, "America," we have
been the black oil bubbling beneath the soil—
not the bottom soil, the bedrock, no,
the oil beneath it—*three fifths of a human being.*
Through centuries of struggle, toil, sacrifice, we arose,
with our blood, to the black bottom soil. Through
three and a half centuries, we have inched
our way, but always being the Shadow, the lowest
of the low. Because this structure we climbed through
was the vicious, murderous Anglo-American mind.
Like Sisyphus, we had our infamous rock; though
Douglas, Delaney, Tubman, and Ida Wells
might've imagined Prometheus chained to the evil
Rock of Color. Mainly though, we endured, and in
surviving, created some of the World's greatest Art—
today's Blues, Jazz, Gospel and Soul, birthing
a new Paradigm for human survival.

Collectively, we were a Role Model for transforming
blood, pain, and death into Jazz-Art-Renaissance.
Dialectical Transformation, lead into golden wonder.
Always the voices of our Djalis (griots) led us, lit our
Paths, whether as Johnson's "God's Trombones," or
the trumpet blasts of Garvey, Dr. King, or Malcolm X.
The suffering, Dialectical Transformation, and
the sacred/secular Djalis, Ma Rainey, Joe Williams,
Aretha, Mahalia, Odetta, Robeson, Jeremiah Wright.
Djalis, embodying Ancestor voices…*Reverend Wright*
is like my community; I could no more renounce him
than renounce my family. Ancestor voices.
God speaking through the flesh; from the bubbling
oil beneath the soil, oil beneath the bloody bedrock of our Being. Voice of Nat Turner, Frederick

Douglass' Fourth of July, Malcolm X's "The Ballot
Or the Bullet"; expressing Dr. King's Vietnam,
American Nightmares, Toni Morrison's "Playing in
The Dark." Renounce your Ancestor voices at a
Terrible price. *Beware the Furies of Apocalypse!*

Notes,   *From "O", an Urban Folk-epic (work-in-progress).
Nefertari, Nefertiti, famous historic Queens of Kemetic, Nile Valley African
Antiquity. Queen Ahmose-Nefertari with her husband Ahmose liberated Kemet
from the Hyksos, Asiatic conquerors. *She was the most venerated queen in Kemet's
history.* Queen Nefertiti was the queen of Ahkenaton, who ruled during Kemet's
New Kingdom Golden Age.

Go! Be a Superhero

I have not seen Muhammad for over a year, but suddenly he is here running alongside the car that I drive, pumping one celebratory fist into the air. He's shouting praises in response to my Barack Obama bumper sticker. He runs so close to my car that I get nervous and pull over to the curb. He is slimmer than I remember with longer hair and thicker eyelashes. Although his cheekbones have sharpened and his voice is in a lower register, he is still not mature. He looks androgynous in the way of eleven-year-old boys. I sense the man that he will become, though; he lurks like pond life just behind the boyish eyes.

"Where have you been?" I ask him.

"I've been around. At school mostly," he says. "I go to Bogle now, just up the street."

When I first met Muhammad he was a chubby nine year old who had moved into our neighborhood with his mom. He attended a Phoenix charter school that specialized in science and technology. Muhammad was three years older than my son. Our houses sat at a diagonal across a typical, East Valley street. We had the basketball hoop. He had the swimming pool. Both houses had trampolines.

Muhammad and my son had this in common as well: both boys were unequivocal geeks. They collected comic books. They both liked archaeology and science experiments that involved insects. They loved video games, and they went through game systems as fast as the technology advanced. Many days they would sit in my living room, their backs hunched over electronic devices, trying to muster the concentration that it took to get to the next level. They'd have discussions bordering on dissertations about the attributes of Bakugan and Pokemon characters.

I liked Muhammad in all of his geeky glory. I also appreciated that he was well-mannered, even though that was no longer in style. He said "yes, ma'am," "no, ma'am," "please," and "thank you." When he saw me with groceries he'd help me carry the bags inside while the other neighborhood boys stood around in the street.

In the universe of kids, however, having manners holds zero cachet.

Muhammad had problems fitting in. His problems may have had something to do with his nerdiness or his weight, but over time I became convinced that it was related to his ethnicity, religion, and to class distinctions. No one wants to be the exotic kid, but that's exactly how people viewed Muhammad. At a time when Muslims were portrayed in the media as dark-skinned terrorists, here was a Muslim boy named after the Islamic prophet, who looked white and whose mother was white. Muhammad's father, who was Middle Eastern, was not around.

It did not help, either, that Muhammad's mother embraced a working class ethos that was at odds with the self-indulgent values of suburbia. She worked and went to school which meant that she was tired by the time she returned home. When Muhammad's mother was napping or doing homework she didn't allow kids to play at her house. She did not hire a landscaper like many of our neighbors, instead Muhammad cut the grass. She drove an old car that had out-of-state license plates and that lacked air conditioning. And because changing your family's schedule is hard as a single parent, she kept Muhammad enrolled at the science school for a year, which didn't help him make friends where he lived.

Muhammad's problems became clear to me one evening in 2006 when a neighbor appeared unannounced at my door. It was right before sunset and the sky was in a dramatic flux, the horizon streaked with oranges, blues, pinks, violets. "Can I talk to you for a minute?" the neighbor whispered through the screen.

"Come on in," I said.

We stood on the small tiled floor at the entrance to my house. "Is your kid going to Muhammad's sleepover?" she asked, still whispering. I decided to lower my voice, too. We were discussing the very serious matter of sleepovers.

"Yes," I whispered, "my kid's spending the night at Muhammad's."

She told me that a car on our street had been vandalized overnight and that someone said nine-year-old Muhammad was responsible. At first I thought it was a joke, but then she repeated rumors that my son had shared with me. People were saying Muhammad was a bully, that he used dirty language. Muhammad's older brother was supposedly in juvenile detention.

I stood for a minute in shocked silence. If people were saying this about Muhammad, what were they saying about my black family? I told the neighbor what I'd told my son: to base her opinions on her personal experiences with the boy. She ended up sending her son to Muhammad's party, but he was not allowed to spend the night.

I witnessed small cruelties performed at Muhammad's expense. A few kids would run and hide when Muhammad came outside. Muhammad kept coming around, believing that this was a game and that he was just being asked to chase them. They upped the ante. They began telling him, straight up, that their parents forbid them to play with him. For weeks, Muhammad still went to their homes. He knew other boys were gathered inside. The parents would tell him that there were "too many kids" in the house. Sometimes they did not answer the door.

After a while, I stopped seeing Muhammad outside. He played at our house and at a couple other houses, but not as often.

The next time I saw him it was spring 2008, and he was running alongside my car.

He talked to me for half an hour that day about Barack Obama's candidacy. Did I know that Obama's father had been Muslim and that Obama would end the war and save the environment? He was excited as he rattled off political facts and he spoke with a sense of purpose.

He also gushed with the nerd-speak that I loved. "Have you seen the t-shirt with Obama in the Superman suit," he asked, "where he's holding the flag on the White House lawn?" he added.

Before that day, I cringed at the iconography that portrayed Obama as a pop culture product or superhero. Those images were everywhere—on posters, t-shirts, comic books. The images seemed too simple; they were a reductive representation of a thoughtful and complex man. But then I watched Muhammad, whose struggle with identity was so similar to Obama's, respond in a positive way to that iconography. Obama as Superhero spoke to Muhammad in a language that was familiar. Muhammad had been marginalized in our community for reasons that maybe he did not fully understand. But as a fanboy, he understood the narrative arc of a superhero. He immediately recognized Obama as someone who could overcome the odds, and that was enough identification for him to hook his young fate to.

The Halloween before the election our streets were crammed with revelers. My son, who was then eight, dressed somewhat predictably as a ninja in all black. It was a better costume than the year before, when his too-small Spiderman outfit looked like he'd dressed in bright blue, spandex pedal-pushers. Muhammad, on the other hand, chose a more sophisticated costume. He wore a John McCain mask and an Obama campaign t-shirt. I read his costume as saying, "Even John McCain is a Barack Obama supporter." It was a funny and subversive message like something you would see on South Park. "A vote for McCain is a vote for the same!" Muhammad squawked from behind his mask. To the consternation of some parents, he said this all night instead of "Trick or treat."

On the day that Obama was elected as the 44th president of the United States, I arrived at my polling place around six-thirty in the morning. Already a hundred people stood in line. Muhammad, who had just turned twelve, stood next to his mom in the middle of the line. He wore an Obama sticker affixed to his t-shirt. When he saw me, he grinned and waved. Although he was too young to vote, he did not look out of place. In fact, he looked like he had figured everything out.

PATRICIA SMITH

Man, Roll the Window Down!

On a slushed side street in the Bronx, a determined hustler
attacks your smudged windshield with enterprise, sloshes
the pane with old water and rocks a feverish squeegee
before you can mouth the word *no.* Stunned at a sluggish
stoplight, you have no choice but to force a smile, nod idly
while he stretches the busy machine of his body across
your hood and whips the gritty wet round and around.
It's a second before you notice that his mouth is moving,
that although he leapt to his task without warning, he is
now attempting to converse as men do, to pass the time,
to shoot the shit. You avoid the mouth, choosing instead
to scan the dank street for anything. There is lots to see—
stands tiled with cheap neon skullcaps, shuttered houses
of praise, the fragrant entrance to Chicken, Ribs & Such,
a city-assed woman drilling her stilettos into concrete,
the butcher shop with price tags pinned to sick meat.
In other words, there is nothing to see. He's still draped
across your Corolla, wiping, squeaking dry and mouthing.
Damned insistent now, he thumps on your windshield
and the light has changed now and behind you drivers
toot elegant *fuck you's.* You scramble for your wallet
because damn it, that's right, hell, you gotta pay the guy
for the gray crisscross swiping that dims the chaos
just enough. But what's the message of that mouth,
he needs you to know something, inside the huge O
of his wild miming there's a collision of collapsed teeth
and you slide your window down to a symphony of horn
and mad street spittle, and your hustler's message,
what he had to get across before he let you pull away
from that street light, *Obama! Obama! Obama! Obama!*
he spurt screeches, his eyes fevered with whiskey

and damn-it-all, no verbs or adornment, just *Obama!*
as if his wiping little life is stuck on triumph, as if
that's all anybody needs to know this day and as he
leans in to roar his one-word stanza, damn the money,
you see that every single one of those teeth, tilted
and pushing for real estate in his mouth, every single
one of them is a gold like you've never seen before.

Brand New Morning

On November 4, 2008, I cast an electoral ballot for the first time in my life. On any level—local, state or national. I was 47 years old, an age at which I should have voted in at least seven presidential elections up until that point. While attending Howard University in the 80s, the idea of voting and participating in an electoral process or government held no importance. The only presidential administration I can remember remotely following came during the Reagan years, mainly because of mandatory sentencing guidelines and the war on drugs. For me, college proved to be a stepping stone for a host of illegal activities centered around the drug culture. The world I operated in, for a significant part of my adult life, did not care about the political fervor of a nation. Everything equated to dollars and cents. To put it bluntly and ashamedly, I did not care who was president, vice president, mayor, or city councilman. I was more preoccupied with going to jail in my self-proclaimed rebellion from the state, which the state happily facilitated in 1997. The government labeled me a convicted felon that year for crimes which I do not contest my guilt. I consistently made bad moral judgments contradictory to the upbringing I received in a two-parent home in which both my parents were educators.

Going to prison proved to be the best thing that ever happened, mainly because it steered me off the path I was headed. The next progression in my development, had I stayed on that path, would have been death. However, I knew that once I reintegrated back into society from prison, I would have the motivation to prove all those people wrong who thought I would amount to nothing. I will never forget hearing the prosecuting attorney at my sentencing tell the judge I didn't deserve a second chance. When Roxbury Correctional Institution released me in 2000, I mistakenly believed my debt had been paid. Soon I would find out the kind of debt I paid isn't easily erased in the consciousness of America.

Prison and the government had given me a check to cash, and just like Martin Luther King, Jr. had noted nearly forty years earlier, there were insufficient funds. This attitude seemed to confirm my complex relationship with America that began in the third grade. To this day, I remember a defiant little white girl who kicked me in the stomach on the playground when I tried to retrieve an errant football. Then she called me the n-word. After I almost broke her jaw and blood splattered on her face, the school officials wanted to expel me. I simply had done what my mother taught me to do. If someone hits you, you hit them back. The school proceeding as to whether I should be expelled or not perplexed me as I thought I was the victim, the one who had been called a terrible name and abused physically. Growing up in Birmingham, Alabama, in the 60s and 70s, I had to understand blackness in the way a kid shouldn't have to. Then too, I had compounded the dilemma by operating on the other side of the law, and in the end, after causing embarrassment to not only my family, but my race as well, I stood in the inglorious irony of it all and began to climb out of the hole I had dug for myself.

After prison, I returned to college and got a BA, MFA and a PhD. I decided if I wanted to atone for the wrongs I had done to my family and others, I needed to educate myself to fully understand the underlining psychosis of our country. I believed that education could help me overcome the stigma of being a convicted felon, even though I would never be able to educate myself enough to not check the box on the application that asked the magic question: "Are you a convicted felon?" But I could be prepared. There were many stumbling blocks I overcame. However, none proved greater than when I walked across Lincoln Park in Albany, New York, to the voting precinct I had been assigned, gave my name, showed my identification and closed the curtain. There was a nervousness about the situation, as if someone might be playing a trick. First of all, I was voting for an African American, and then too, I had begun to believe I could actually catch the sprit of Western Civilization, convicted felon and all. I'd never in my life had that feeling. I mean never, ever. Before I pulled the switch, I thought about my maternal grandmother and paternal grandfather who had lived in Alabama all of their lives. My mother and father were the result of my grandparents' willingness to sacrifice so that their children would have a better life. My parents had done the same for me and my sister, yet I had almost thrown it all away. While I understood the historicity of the moment, it really didn't hit me until I woke up the next morning. After a long night during which Barak Obama was confirmed the 44th

President of the United States, I checked my email and a friend from California made an interesting declaration. That morning he had gotten out of his bed to buy a red, white and blue American flag. He took the flag and put it on his porch. The email went on to talk about how proud he was that day to be an American.

Only a few months earlier Michelle Obama received harsh criticism for saying those exact words. Certain segments of America gasped in horror and "oh my god's" as to how any African American could not be totally unflinching in their loyalty to the United States. Excuse me. Slavery? Segregation? The continuing need for affirmative action? The list could go on, really. However, people from African American communities understood sister-girl perfectly. The mere audacity that African Americans did not understand Michelle Obama, or privately or aloud say amen to her provocative statement is utterly insane. Many African Americans are still walking around with that insufficient funds check in their pocket, trying to make some sense of a country their ancestors helped build, but have always had to take a back seat or fight long and hard when it came to addressing issues concerning its well-being. The question within my circle of friends became: how can we be totally proud of a country where there are so many hidden barriers and boundaries still in place? My friends wanted to know why African Americans always have to be the one lowering their heads, forgiving and not getting? Why are we perceived as racist when we scream race is a factor? This is the underlying discussion in African American communities that is often hidden from the white segment of America. Barack Obama becoming president helped to ease wounds like these that have not totally healed. The image of a black man seated in the most powerful position in the world helps to send a message of hope and possibility.

After I read the email my friend sent, I went to the college campus where I teach nowadays and saw the impact one man can have on a people. First of all, every African American I encountered that day seemed to walk a little smoother—as if they were doing the James Brown "Camel Walk"— their chest poked out a little further, their smile widened to the ears. One of only a few African American professors at my college ran into me in the copier room and gave me the coded smile, like "yeah, we did it." We gave each other the confirming head nod not without saying a word. On this day, the African American community proved to be a collective (we), not monolithic, but (we). November 3rd came and it was truly a brand new morning. All those years of having to moan had given us Obama. As an African American, I have always been suspicious and untrusting of my country. In fact, I don't know if I have ever said "my country" in a caring context. Don't get me wrong, I understood that I live in a country that offers certain liberties I can't find anywhere else, but historicity and the polemic nature of the past is a hard situation to outrun.

With that said, I will state I misjudged the impact of what an image can perpetuate to this country. When Obama was in the heat of his presidential race, I listened intently within my own community of friends and family to people who seemed obsessed with the image of a black man as president. I wanted a black president, and yes, I understood we would have to share him, that he was everybody's president, but still, I wanted him to win. What I didn't want to happen was for African Americans to get so caught up in the image that they were willing to sacrifice or make certain concessions in regards to blackness and historical fact, or the sobering reality of race still faced in this country. In order to gain the presidency, Obama had to tightrope the issues of race and oftentimes ignore the black community. He couldn't be biased and prejudicial in his campaign. I have to grant that it took a special man to run the campaign he ran, and for that he has my utmost respect.

The image of a black president hit me like a Joe Louis punch when I exited the Capitol South metro stop in Washington, DC, on January 20, 2009, at around eight in the morning. I spent most of my adult life in Washington. I had gone to the Martin Luther King, Jr. holiday march with Stevie Wonder singing *Happy Birthday* in the early 80s. Then too, I had been at the Million Man March in the 90s. However, those two events in consecutive decades paled in comparison to what Obama's election in the new millennium had achieved. The streets were choked with literally tens of thousands of people in every direction. Intensity in the air so thick you could cut it with a knife. Every acronym of law enforcement revealed in the block lettering on the back of their windbreakers. On the sidewalks strangers struck up conversations with each other on whims. I met a Hispanic guy from the lower panhandle of Texas who had traveled to DC just for this moment.

Walking down Constitution Avenue, we centered our conversation on the hope and new found love for our country. I saw more than one elderly person walking on two canes, pulling and willing themselves forward to be a part of this historic occasion. Obama had cauterized the racial divide—if only for a moment—and at a moment's notice people wanted to see this man make history. My silver coded ticket enabled me to watch the swearing in next to the Reflecting Pool. I stood genuflecting the moment, having overcome my own personal tragedies to be present. I took a deep breath and looked back at a sea of Americans of all hues in my brown pupils. The corridor of human bodies ran effortlessly past the Washington Monument. I was humbled to be in the presence of history. Obama's image brought people together in the hopes we can work out our differences.

My mother and I attended the Southern States ball that night. In many ways, Obama's election was helping to bring us closer together. I had disappointed her terribly over the years, squandering my potential, living a life no mother could be proud of for her son. I strained our relationship with my unacceptable behavior, but just like a mother's unyielding love for her offspring, she provided the support I needed to right the ship I had wrecked. Now we were zipping around town attending inauguration gatherings and enjoying the hopeful buzz that ran through DC with kinetic-like energy. It meant everything in the world to be able to share that moment with the woman who had been the toughest on me when I needed it the most. She refused to condone any of the behavior I had done and now she was my biggest advocate. We both were dressed in after-five attire. I could not help but get caught up in the moment. My mother moves with ease and grace through events like those, having been president of the Alabama Education Association and a delegate for the National Education Association for years. Washington is a place she loves to frequent, yet all the years that I stayed in DC, we had never spent time like we did during the inauguration. The election and consequent swearing in of Barack Obama helped me to understand that change is possible if you are willingto see the race to the end. I don't know if I will ever get that feeling that I had that entire week I was back in Washington. From Barack to my mother, I left feeling that I was part of something—a country, a nation.

Obama Shuffle

we move as if chained together
we move like we are pacing out the complex steps
to the new line dance

thank you for taking off work today, for standing
outside, in the cold, on heels, flats and sore feet for hours
bundled in winter scarves, long skirts, leather coats,
faux fur, bandanas, business suits, fatigues, sweats and jeans
clutching designer purses, book bags and each other

to the right, to the right, to the right, to the right

thank you for clearing your throat
when anybody forgot to move the line

thank you for leaning on your canes
for looking over your reading glasses

to the left, to the left, to the left, to the left

for casting a watchful eye at the poll workers
and at me and at everybody within squinting distance

for wearing my mother's nose on your faces, for wearing
her shoes, for standing with your hands on your hips too

now kick, now kick, now kick, now kick

now move as if chained together, move like we are
pacing out the complex steps to the new line dance
to our new history, stride into the voting booth

now walk it by yourself, now walk it by yourself

JASMINE GUY

On the Road '08
A Speech for the Obama Campaign

I am an actor, a dancer, a performer. People are used to seeing me speak words and become a character from the pages of a script. But today I'm not pretending I am someone else nor are my words from someone else. Today I'm just me, speaking to you humbly as a woman who,...well let me just tell you where I was raised and how I grew up. My family moved to Atlanta from Port Chester, New York, when I was seven. My parents were teachers and we lived across the street from Morehouse College where my father taught. I grew up around six black colleges: Morehouse College, Spelman College, The Interdenominational Theological Center, Clark College, Morris Brown College and Atlanta University.

As a child, I met and knew Hank Aaron, Julian Bond, Andrew Young, Hosea Williams and Maynard Jackson, their kids and their families. I grew up in a city of thinkers and doers, professionals and workers. I grew up in King Country where educated, political, well read, ambitious black folk weren't an anomaly. It was normal and fair to do things with your life. It was expected of you and nurtured into you and as right as rain. So when I met Barack Obama, he was familiar to me. During this campaign we've heard some say of Obama, "He's different, he's not like the others." But he's not a freak of nature or some exotic, odd black man who came out of nowhere. He was a man I had seen in many men before him. He was like my father, a Morehouse graduate, who went on to Howard Divinity School and Columbia University, or my uncle Wendell Whalum, organist, composer, director of Morehouse's music department and glee club for decades. Obama is as familiar as Benjamin E. Mays, Thurgood Marshall, A. Philip Randolph and W.E.B. DuBois.

Knowing him is important, but it is also important to know

where we come from. When I get a chance to speak at schools, I tell kids all the time, specifically, who and what they come from. Yes, Muhammad Ali, but also Jack Johnson. Yes, Shirley Franklin, but also Shirley Chisholm. Yes, Malcolm X, but also Marcus Garvey. Yes Jay Z, but also Langston Hughes.

We are Americans with a rich, unique experience as blacks that cannot be extricated from the fabric of this country. No matter how many lies are told or stories omitted, it lives in our collective spirit. Obama is a bi-racial black person like a lot of folk I know. He brings to the table a magnificent perspective, but that perspective is only part of it. He will be president because of his mind, his character and ability.... And I'm sorry, I feet something. Sorry, I got emotional because I didn't think this was going to happen while I was still here. I hoped maybe my daughter would see it, but I didn't think I would recognize our next president, that he or she would be this familiar to me. I got used to being ignored these past eight years. I gave in to being embarrassed by our choice for president. And yes, *we* put President Bush back in office in the last election. It shouldn't have been that close to begin with. But for whatever reason we did, we are here now, with egg on our face. Now what you going to do? I asked myself. Now you got someone you believe in. What you going to do? *Now.*

I'm going to speak up for him, travel for him and reach out to others to do what they can do. We have to go beyond what we usually do. We have to go past our own kitchen tables. We must vote, get others to vote and talk about stuff we usually avoid. Phenomenal change in me, in us, must happen. I just want us to get up! This won't happen while we sit on the couch. This requires participation. Let's talk about your reservations. Let's talk about your fears. Let's talk about the issues that concern you. I can't dictate who you vote for, but we can't sit this one out. We must be a part of this.

I believe in Obama. He is a candidate with character, with morals and standards and a global view that puts us in context with the rest of the world, not set apart. He exudes integrity and a beautiful blend of pride and humility, focus and intuition, trust and conviction. And I believe Barack holds himself accountable to his family, his community, his mother and grandmother, his wife and ultimately to us. That's how he's built. He takes responsibility and expects accountability. Up until now it's just been a boys' club up there in Washington, a country club we can't get into; a party we're not invited to and not because we are black, but because we are the people.

The people have been locked out. I've never seen mistakes and travesties of the magnitude we've witnessed these last eight years occur without heads rolling. But I have seen that the boys look out for each other. They're boys from way back. Homeboys of homeboys for generations and we are out here looking in. That's *our* government ain't it? Well let's get back in there. Let's be heard. Let's be seen and represented for who we really are and what we really want in life and how we really want to live.

44, Sacred and Rising

You straddle the horizon
like Legba cresting a hill:
one foot in the absolute,
the other steeped in duende.

We danced with your reflection
as camera flashes questioned
your right to knife-fight
with blood money and history:

Some swore Mt. Kenya birthed
you in light, erupting bell
and djembe, dark loam
stamped beneath naked feet;

Others cried too much Irish
granite in your skin, that
Cyrillics raged in your blood,
prophesizing rain and hail.

Night & Day, we sliced you
to marrow, down to the scripture
of each oaken ring, down to
the demitasse of bone and gristle.

Until we discovered you, Barack,
mounted upon a chariot, riding
head high; juggernaut rippling
through the hoarfrost of dawn.

What I Saw Shining on My Mother's Face

It was no small matter to be canvassing in my small, Midwestern town with my white mother, a few days before Obama's election. My mother and father were married in Guam, two years after the passing of *Loving v. State of Virginia*, and in the years following their return to the states there was no shortage of "incidents," though they never spoke of them when my brother and I were children. Predictable stuff: some (luckily very few) family members condemning the marriage (though it's a kind of visual cliché, it happened: my mother's grandmother, after shaking my father's hand, wiping her own on her apron); other family members and friends "concerned" with the psychological welfare of their future kids; apartments available, but not available to them; people publically questioning, with words or looks, whether or not her brown babies were actually hers (which, in response to one of these in a supermarket, she yelled, "Yes they're mine, and I have the stretch marks to prove it!"); her son coming home from collecting for his paper route where one of his customers, drunk and enraged that the boy was walking with his white female friend, chased him down the block screaming "Don't walk around here with white girls, Nigger!" All that said, ours was a home where race, though abundantly *there*, was almost never spoken of.

In fact, I can recall only very few overt mentions of race from either my mother or father, the latter of whom made a comment to me, a jaded and weary aside about a black man on trial: "I can guess how this will go." But from neither of them did I ever hear anything explicit, anything remotely like "Here's how my heart's been broken by this country, my friends, my family…." Nothing like it.

And so there we were, knocking on doors in my small town, my mother holding the list of street names. "Is this Washington? Nope, this is Lincoln. Okay, we have to do about 10 houses on Lincoln and it looks like about 25 on Washington." Though the street names are too good to be true, they're true. We parked on Washington and hoofed it from there. My white mother holding the map while she and her son knocked on doors for a bi-racial African-American man running for president.

For the most part my mother's not really the type to go on about how she feels. This doesn't negate the fact that she's brave and articulate about her feelings—which I learned as we mourned my father's death—but she's practical to the core, and I think some of her pragmatism makes the kind of emotional analysis I favor a bit, well, *simple,* as they might say in Verndale, Minnesota (pop. 559), where she's from. Such that spending a bundle of time wondering why the drunk chased you down the block calling you nigger wasn't going to put food on the table. Nor would it make you very happy. I think I get it.

Which is why I want to say what I saw shining in my mother's face as we returned home, pretty tired from the work we put in canvassing, and we came upon a line of people that stretched from an early polling booth to the end of this city block, turning the corner, heading up to the next street, while not one but *two* bands played some version of country music for the people waiting in line, this very Obama strong line, festive and multi-generational and multi-ethnic and multi-classed. Looking at this with her son. Yes, that's what I want to say. What I saw shining there in my mother's face.

Michelle Obama: Woman of Power

Michelle Obama would be a very powerful woman, even if she had not fallen in love with a man whose vision for his life and his country pulled her into the glare of a brighter spotlight than she might have chosen on her own. Emanating from her seemingly effortless ability to be simultaneously the new America and the old neighborhood, her power is not something she wields. It's something she *is*. She represents much more than a new idea about what a *First Lady* might be, she represents a very old idea about what *America* itself can be: *one nation, under God, indivisible, with liberty and justice for all.*

Her power reflects an America that we consciously changed through years of protest and sacrifice and determination, in order to be able to participate fully. Not just as black folks, not just as women, but as citizens. Because even though Michelle and her brother, Craig, might not have known it at the time, that's what Fraser and Marian Robinson were raising over there on Chicago's south side, citizens of a brand new world. Michelle Obama is a surprise only because we have been so busy struggling to make things right that we didn't notice the fruits of our labors were already hanging heavy in the trees and the harvest was at hand.

Michelle is living proof, not of America's mythical perfection, but of America's actual possibilities, paid for since its inception by the blood of citizens of all races and genders and religions and points of view who believed that this would be a very special place if we could just bring its realities into line with all those beautiful words upon which it was founded: *We hold these truths to be self-evident, that all men are created equal.*

Michelle Obama's power is that she is the one who allows *us* to expand into the *we*. To finally exhale all those years of exclusion and anger and frustration and look around at this amazing, frustrating, strange, deluded, beautiful country of which we are such a deeply important part, and feel for the first time a deep down stirring in our souls that means it is now, finally, gloriously officially our own, with all its problems to solve and complicated histories to understand.

Michelle Obama is the best of us, the new Americans. The ones the nation and the world are waiting for with an anticipation almost as great as our own. Alice Walker says, "Remember, you, yourself, are America." I think Michelle Obama is who she means.

OPAL MOORE

Transcendence: Thoughts on Love and Race

"One of the most prevalent media messages about Obama is that he "transcends race," or something to that effect. *Newsweek* (12/25/06) said he is "sometimes described as 'post-racial.'"
　　　　　—Peter Hart, *FAIR* (Fairness and Accuracy in Reporting), April 2007

"Now that a black man from a broken home has become President of the United States, no black child has an excuse for failure."
　　　　　—Blog response to Obama election.

"I don't want his [Obama's] plans to succeed... I hope he fails."
　　　　　—Rush Limbaugh, January 16, 2009

"In things racial we have always been, and I believe continue to be, in too many ways essentially a nation of cowards."
　　　　　—Eric Holder, Attorney General

Multiple choice question: If a black man and a black woman marry (each other):
　　　a. they have both transcended race
　　　b. they are both racists
　　　c. they are unambitious
　　　d. trick question: it is the 1950s and they have no
　　　　　other choice
　　　e. they are color blind

Multiple choice question: If a white man and a white woman marry (each other):
　　　a. they are normal
　　　b. they are all-American

c. they love each other
d. they are compatible
e. white is not a color

A survey of claims made about Barack Obama and his election to the office of President of the United States (as well as the fact that he is happily married to a successful African American woman from the Southside of Chicago) would provide a thorough portrait of the racial anxieties and posturing of contemporary Americans. The whimsical multiple choice questions (above) are in the spirit of Patricia Williams's challenge of the media usage of "transcendence" when she asked, "What would it reveal about the hidden valuations of race if one were to invert the equation by positing that Barack Obama 'transcended' whiteness because his father was black?" (*The Nation*, March 2007)

What does it mean to 'transcend' race? Is it supposed to mean that Obama discovered how to thrive in a racist society while being preternaturally unaware of race and the significations of race? Is it to mean that white people can forgive him his color if he "signs" whiteness rather than blackness? If the latter, what are the "signs" of whiteness?

Political scientist Manning Marable suggests that Obama's post-racialism is a strategy to side-step American racism. In *The Great Wells of Democracy: The Meaning of Race in American Life* (2002), Marable observes an inverse correlation between a black politician gaining white votes and the density of the local black population. In other words, a black politician's success in garnering white votes was predictable based on the number of black people voting for that candidate in the voting district—the more white votes gained, the fewer black voters supporting that candidate in the district. Marable defines post-racial politics as a politics that accepts the impossibility of black people successfully petitioning as an interest group in the U.S. The winning strategy? —black politicians will not be permitted to align themselves with any social justice agenda *initiated or embraced by an organization perceived to be led or endorsed by blacks* and win white votes, regardless of the benefit of the proffered social or economic policies to white voters.

Various media pundits have tried to tease out their own "hidden valuations of race," attempting to explain the "appeal" of Obama (why oh why do we love him so!) as deriving from his non-slavery, non-civil rights tinged ancestry (his Kenyan ancestry is conceived as politics-free, slavery being characterized as local); his upbringing in a white household; his exotic past (Hawaii and Indonesia), etc. Few refer to Obama's own recollections shared in his memoir, *Dreams From My Father* (1995). In this first book, he relates the difficulties he faced in shaping his own personal and political identity; how he sought out readings in African American literature and history in his search for a better understanding of himself and the complications of his American story and existence. He eloquently explores his discovery of the importance of black community to his own emotional growth and intellectual grounding.

Indeed, when it comes to Obama's successful bid for the presidency, we must tease out the "hidden valuations of race," the extant notions of race, power, and love that have left American voters both anxious and thrilled about their support of Obama; as they celebrate the importance of the election of the first black president, yet struggle to strip him of his race, his heritage, his ethical grounding and sense of fairness, his regard for the lessons we should have learned during the Civil Rights Movement struggle and other economic struggles around the world.

The Rush Limbaugh crowd will continue to keep it simple: they hate Obama and would rather see the entire country crumble to its foundations than have him "win." The pundits who continue to slaver over Obama might be broken hearted to realize that Obama, according to Marable, "played" them. And that black people played along, understanding the courtship dance Obama would have to perform in order to win the chance to take us beyond Dr. King's "I Have A Dream" speech, and one small step closer to the realization of democracy. If this presidency inspires us to revisit our better selves, we will all have constructed a far more powerful and lasting emblem than a 21st century "black is beautiful" t-shirt.

What is transcendence? In this country, transcendence is the "sign" of whiteness? And the sign of whiteness is being a winner. For as long as Obama is perceived to be winning—staying ahead in the polls, getting his legislation through Congress, drawing the respect of international leaders— he can be taken to the bosom of white Americans who actually seem to miss being loved by the black caretakers they lost with the end of slavery.

As one pundit observed, by loving Obama, white America can love itself once more. Even more important, black Americans can as well.

As for the Limbaugh crowd, with any luck, they will become our new minority.

jessica CARE moore

Barack Obama & the State of Black Women in Love

For my mother who said after over 40 years of resistance, and the heartbreak of the 60s riots, Kennedy and King assassinations, she would finally consider becoming an American.

It's difficult to have a love affair with your country.
When you've been portrayed as its mammy.
The caretaker of the country's children, but not the woman
          of the house.

A house built with your ancestors' hands
Painted white and shadowed by blood stained windows.
A peculiar institution with your body as witness
Classrooms of misinformation running as the bell rings
Under your armpits
Through your nostrils
Out your throat
Between your toes.

The birthplace of dance.
Jazz. Tap. Hip Hop.

Your native feet never needed to be discovered.
They were already connected to a place. This land
Is your land. This land was already my land.

I carry a red and blue earth friendly tote
With the words HOPE written in white
To hold my son's diapers now.

This is peculiar for me.
A few years ago, someone, a fellow poet, a friend,

An activist would've asked.

Why so patriotic, jess?

It's naïve to think the revolution has arrived
That all is well!
Children are being bombed
In Palestine
As I write this poem.

It is still a revolutionary act
To simply love.
To hope?
I don't want to die and leave my son
Fiery words & no peace.

I don't want him to rewrite the same poems
In my same voice
Thirty years after my work is considered the
Past.

The same way they say our writing sounds like
The Black Arts Movement.
Because not much has
Moved in this country.

Has it?

Since Jim Crow on the Race Riots or
Facebook or Myspace or Amadou or
The Jena 6.

Until now, maybe.

I watch the pearls around Michelle's neck
I imagine them as cowry shells
She is long and regal and beautiful and brown.
Tall as Masai Women painted red.

I know President Barack Obama sees this
And this makes me love
The idea of him.

Even more.

Him. Kenyan and American rooted.
Knowing himself and loving himself enough
To not be swayed by Harvard so much.
That he would forget what he would really need
Grassroots activism and a comrade
Who loved him

To get him to a higher place.

She is more than our generation's Jackie O.
An unapologetically brilliant woman with daughters
As wings
& husband as Chief.

This is a new American story
I am not ashamed to pass down.

For the first time I am inspired to imagine
The possibility of an Inaugural poem.

I am too revolutionary, I am told. Perhaps?
But, I don't listen to those words.

I have lived my life in the triality
of many Americas.
As Native. As Ancestor. Mother. Pioneer. Griot.
Warrior. Holder of secrets. Lover. International
Representative. Cook.

Who better than the daughters of Harriet and Ida
Coretta and Betty?
Phyllis and Billie?

Someone might have told a young Obama
His life wasn't possible.

So, how can I not imagine a poem?

I'm sure Michelle wasn't
Always confident she would find a loyal
Man to share her life with.
None of this is certain. And it doesn't matter
Who read the poem that day.

But wouldn't it be perfect in the ancestral air of sonia?
Or the grace of   ruby
The blues of   jayne
The hurricane of   asha
The imagery of   pearl
The spitfire of   nikki

Who better to write about it
& tell the world about
How we feel?

About the image of those beautiful smiling girls
In pigtails and twists as their mom and
Their dad enter a sacred space
Many of us had written off as impossible
Or hoped for in our
Grandchildren's lifetime.
Not today.

Being inspired to even consider writing
A poem, an homage for an American
President and his family in my lifetime
Has shown me the possibility of what can
Truly be manifested beyond dreams.

I am told today that the moon aligned itself
With Jupiter and Uranus and it won't happen again

Until 2052.
I believe that life & exact science & astrology can be
Altered when God decides to make it so.
And while many are celebrating a first
In America's History

I am quietly chanting

Welcome Home
Welcome Home Barack
Welcome Home Michelle
Welcome back those at War
Welcome Back to America

Langston's America
El Hajj Malik El Shabazz's America
Martin's Dream of America
My blue collar mother and
Cement laying daddy's
America.

We have work to do.
And many things to
Un/do.
In the midst of so many uncertain days
In this place called America.

And like so many women in love.
At times I still thought I was alone
Days after the inauguration
At awkward moments
Tears would just come
While watching the news
Seeing that mall.
Watching them dance
After hearing my 2-year old
King scream
Obaaaaaama!

Until I began asking other women
Many of them single moms.
In private, they say, yes!
It is happening to them too.

Perhaps he is the father
Of a New America.

I know I feel the heart of this
Country beating again.
Just enough life & breath and hope
To make our historical blues
seem less in vain.

As the night essence of white stars
Finally fall
        touching the ground

And finding the hearts of

Women

Of men
Of children

Of we
the people

CHUCK D AND GAYE THERESA JOHNSON

From 40 Acres to 8 Cents: A Married Couple's Ruminations on the Symbolism of Barack Obama

We're hard pressed to think of a time when Black people have been more popular. Barack Obama has lent an important credibility to Blackness that has real currency for many of us. The visibility of people of color, progressive whites, and women in the president's cabinet promises to lend a new legitimacy to our qualifications as leaders and social citizens. This was our first thought as we perused the availability of posters of Obama in an outdoor marketplace not long ago. We were among many couples that Saturday, enjoying what we feel is an essential tradition for community interaction all over the world. We bantered about the deflation of difference in the U.S. between selling something "hot" and selling something meaningful, about who determines that meaning, and at what cost. We were trying to settle on an Obama poster to hang in our home, acknowledging that since King and Kennedy, there have been few significant social figures whose pictures our communities would consider displaying on a wall, let alone in their homes.

There were many shapes and sizes, various drawn, photographed, painted, some computer-created configurations of Obama; some with Michelle, and some of the whole family. In the end, we decided to purchase something by our friend, political artist Shepard Fairey, whose HOPE campaign series inspired both acknowledgment from Obama himself and the ire of the Associated Press. Shepard's profound articulations of social justice, struggle, and love mean a lot to us, especially because we know that this is a combination that is worthy of sustained commitment, and we know that HOPE does not sustain itself. It needs us now more than ever.

We got our picture framed. And when it came time to hang it, we stared at it together, contemplating where to display one of the most significant people—and events—of our mutual lifetimes. The living room? Our office? We felt that our choice might echo a long-held tradition among Blackfolk, whose collective agreement on "people and moments of great magnitude" (King, Washington, Kennedy, and others) hung in parlors, kitchens, and living rooms. We recalled Oscar Micheaux's *Body and Soul* starring the great Paul Robeson, in which a picture of Booker T. Washington served as the most prominent symbol in the most significant scenes of the film.

We decided that *where* we hung this poster could reveal its symbolic significance to us as a people, as a married couple, and as human beings. Where should we place this, not only in our home, but in our minds, and eventually, in our own political activities? We return to what we know: that Black people have never been more popular than they are now, which means that as we hang this poster, we are living in a new racial and social context.

Our images are everywhere, but Black people are also more popular than ever in *unwanted* ways. According to Human Rights Watch, Blacks were arrested as much as five-and-a-half times more as whites on drug charges every year for the past three decades (the same study found that drug use among Blacks is no higher than it is for whites), yet Blacks go to prison at ten times the rate of whites on those same drug charges.[1] The same kinds of statistics bear out in other areas of society, making Black people and their communities the most "popular" demographic for prison terms, underfunded educational programs, the eradication of after-school programs, and the proliferation of despair. Popular indeed.

How do we account for this disparity in both material condition and symbolic representation? On January 15, 2009, we inaugurated our first Black president. In the same month, United for a Fair Economy reported that the disparity in Black/white wealth has grown to such a degree that people of color have 8 cents for every dollar of *white* wealth. By the end of this recession, economists predict that 33 percent of Blacks and 41 percent of Latinos will likely drop out of the middle class. In nearly half of low-income households, after housing costs are paid, families will have only $257 month for food, $24 for clothing, and $9 for medical care.[2]

We will note two things at this juncture: First, the difference between income and wealth. People use income to meet daily expenses and pay utility bills, but wealth is home equity, pension funds, savings accounts and investments. People inherit wealth and pass it down from generation to

44 ON 44

generation. This is why George Lipsitz makes it plain that whites who out-*earn* Blacks by a 5 to 3 ratio, out-*own* Blacks by a 10 to 1 ratio.[3] People use wealth to send their children to private schools or to give their adult children down payments for homes. And when asked about it, many fail to see any injustice in the differences between their condition and those who have little or no wealth. Sociologist Thomas Shapiro reported that in interviews he did for his book *The Hidden Cost of Being African American*, people who inherited tens or hundreds of thousands of dollars told him that they were self-made and self-reliant. These people "proudly reported how the assets they inherited grew under their stewardship." When they tapped their wealth, it was to deal with emergencies or to take advantage of opportunities—opportunities that usually build more wealth. They did not see how such practices hand today's inequalities on to the next generation.[4]

The second thing we will note is the popularity, notable in the narratives of middle-class people of color, to settle on an easy answer about this disparity: this condition was not created by George W. Bush and is not over with Barack Obama. We will give Bush his due for its renewed strength, the same due we gave his father. But this disparity has been built carefully over hundreds of years. We will likewise refuse, at this juncture, to naturalize racism and inequality as part of the terrain of American democracy.

Returning, then, to the question of the disparity between Black popularity and the collective Black reality, and between the growing popularity of colorblind ideology and color-bound realities, we find a tidy summation of this apparent contradiction in Robin Kelley's description of the effects of unregulated markets in the late 20th century. Kelley concluded that our whole-hearted acceptance of them is in large part responsible for a shrinking labor market and the militarization of urban space, and *also* for the circulation of the very representations of race that generate terror in all of us at the sight of young Black men and yet compel most of America to want to wear their shoes."[5]

As we considered our poster and its eventual place in our home, we acknowledged our belief that as much as this is a question of representation, it has always been a question of history. And to that point, one more prelude must be mentioned: since the announcement of Obama's presidential bid, we have received many inspirational emails connecting this unprecedented racial moment with other, less illustrious moments in history. The latest one we received was the juxtaposition of two pictures, one the famous Norman Rockwell painting, "The Problem We All Live With," depicting national guardsmen in Louisiana escorting Ruby Bridges as she integrated New Orleans public schools in 1960. Next to it was another photo, this one of 6-year-old Sasha Obama being escorted by secret servicemen to her classroom on *her* first day of school. My how things have changed, mused the sender. It was indeed an inspiring juxtaposition, though not without its deep contradictions. We will note that Ruby Bridges' family, from Little Rock, were working class people. The Obama parents went to Harvard, are both attorneys, have enjoyed a well-deserved and substantial salary for their efforts, and wield considerably more power and wealth than, arguably, the entire Black population of Little Rock in 1960. Though we would be fools to think that the Obamas are not in harm's way much of their time, the danger posed in the Rockwell painting, at once as individual as it is deeply reflective of the collective peril in which Black people existed, is nonetheless a different danger than the one in the photo of Sasha Obama. Ruby Bridges remembered that the heckling from the white crowd gathered did not scare her as much as someone in the crowd holding up a black doll in a coffin.

It is indeed a joy to see the distinction, and without detracting too much from the moment (because we, too, want our moment), we must acknowledge that this juxtaposition was somewhat discomfiting for us because of what those who *don't* understand its historical significance are doing to collapse history into snapshots, taking away the long road of struggle that Blacks endured so that Obama might be president. The fact is that today, whites made up 58 percent of the nation's public school enrollment in 2006, but the average white student attended a school that was nearly 80 percent white. African Americans accounted for 17 percent of all students, but the average black student attended a school that was 53 percent black. Latinos made up 19 percent of enrollment but attended schools that were typically 55 percent Latino.[6] With this kind of reality, the narrated differences between the 1960 painting and the 2008 photo become murky.

To that point, there are too many ways in which the visibility of Black progress is being used to justify the eradication of policies and opportunities that assure equality and collective success. Just this year, the

Supreme Court voted to limit the reach of the Voting Rights Act, arguing that it is no longer necessary for any electoral district that is not a majority-minority district to be protected by a provision of the Voting Rights Act. And there is already discussion about whether *Brown v. Board* should come under similar action. The notion is that if we are a nation that can elect a Black president, we must be a nation that can be color blind. Our future remains, however, color-bound.

The notion that Black people in 2009 have only 8 cents per dollar of white wealth inspires remembrance of another numeric reality, this one from 1865: the promise of 40 acres. And like the two snapshots we mentioned, what lies between 40 acres in 1865 and 8 cents in 2009 cannot be realized by only rejoicing in the distinction. We might take, actually, some weighty instruction from that era about how to counter the pervasive colorblindness that is taking shape these days.

In 1861, when Lincoln declared war, Black people saw an opportunity. And even though it was, perhaps, at first no more promising than any other, Blacks were poised to increase the pressures of their long-standing struggles and had the presence of mind to act upon that opportunity. Cedric Robinson writes that "upon Lincoln's pronouncement, slave insurrections broke out in Mississippi and Virginia; an additional 25 conspiracies were reported in Arkansas, Virginia, South Carolina, Louisiana, and Kentucky. Escaped slaves in the lower and upper South made for the nearest union forces. Of the 112,000 slaves in Missouri, 22,000 had escaped by 1862."[7] When emancipation became a reality, albeit dubious, Black people created a new language that W.E.B. Du Bois has called "abolition democracy," and with it fought for the 13th, 14th, and 15th Amendments to the Constitution:

> At the Charleston Black Convention in 1865 they called for more than nominal freedom, they demanded the development of their full being as humans. Between 1865 and 1877 they fashioned alliances with poor whites to elect progressive majorities to office, and their successes led to the first universal public education systems in the South, to governments that subsidized the general economic

infrastructure rather than just the privileges and property of the elite…[T]hey were betrayed by the compromise of 1877, by the removal of federal troops from the South, by the legal consolidation of the combination of sharecropping and Jim Crow Segregation, and by Supreme Court decisions that took protections away from black people and extended them to corporations."[8]

But Black people nonetheless created a language of struggle and freedom that is a valuable precedent, something that we as a couple, but also the broader "we" as people committed to equality in the Obama era, must have the presence of mind to remember.

It would not be wise to forge a comparison between the struggles of the Radical Reconstruction era and our present moment without more lengthy consideration. But let us note that for the current moment under consideration, there are many lessons to be drawn from the presence of mind exercised by Black struggles in that era.

First, they were awake, awake to the contradictions manifest in post-bellum freedom. Second, literacy and the active exercising of rights became incredibly popular. People took advantage of what had been denied to them, and movements in both of these areas proliferated. After 1877, Blacks would not vote again in the south until the Voting Rights Act of 1965. Third, they wasted no time, refused to allow Dixiecrats or even Radical Republicans shape the language or trajectory of what freedom would mean. ithout drawing a direct comparison between 1877 and 2011, what helpful guidelines for our day might lie in these three observations?

Today, to see the labors and sacrifices of civil rights workers, known and unknown, come to some symbolic and material fruition has created inspiration in communities around the world. One of our undertakings, then, should be the exposure of the contradictions of Black "popularity," especially when the material reality of race in America is well hidden underneath rhetorical professions of American universality.

There are a few key things we hope Black people will remain awake to see. First, as we began with, the contradiction between apparent Black success and the reality of the collective experience of poor people and people of color. In 2008, United for a Fair Economy estimated that this sub prime

44 on **44**

loan business will mean a total loss of wealth for people of color between $164 billion and $213 billion, what appears to represent the greatest loss of wealth for people of color in modern US history. Black borrowers alone will lose between $71 billion and $92 billion, and Latino borrowers will lose between $75 billion and $98 billion for the same period. And they further note that homeownership rates for Blacks compared to Whites are already starting to take back recent gains. At the current rate of improvement (from 1970 to 2006), parity will not be achieved for another 5,423 years.[9] Second, we must remain aware of why, even in the midst of these realities, we should be so optimistic about President Obama's election. And would say that it's because we know that it is social movements and grassroots activity that shape outcomes, and we've seen one in this election. History has shown us that people of color have created an extraordinary battery of what Robin Kelley calls "freedom dreams." From demands for 40 acres and a mule to fair housing and equal pay, Robin Kelley conceived *Freedom Dreams* as an effort to recover ideas—"visions fashioned mainly by those marginalized black activists who proposed a different way out of our constrictions." And toward this end, he asks that we remember that "the conditions and the very existence of social movements enable participants to imagine something different, to realize that things need not always be this way."[10] There are many gains to be made because of the victory we have won in the election of Barack Obama.

Even with the contradictions we know we face, with the terrible realities facing so many of our brothers and sisters, we feel we have new reasons for HOPE. We decided to hang our new painting in our living room: it is the center of our home, the place we congregate during family gatherings, the place where we collaborate on some of our best ideas. We think the other faces that have graced the homes of Black folk over the years—King, X, Carver, Du Bois, Kennedy—we think they saw the future in our past. And as we look upon our painting, we recommit ourselves to remembering our past in the future.

(*Atlanta, Georgia 2009*)

Notes

1. "Decades of Disparity: Drug Arrests and Race in the United States." The 2009 Human Rights Watch Report.

2. Amaad Rivera, Jeannette Huezo, Christina Kasica, and Dedrick Muhammed, "Silent Depression: State of the Dream 2009" (Boston, Massachusetts: United For a Fair Economy Annual Report), January 15, 2009.

3. George Lipsitz, *The Possessive Investment in Whiteness: How White People Profit from Identity Politics* (Philadelphia: Temple University Press, 2006), p. 108.

4. Thomas Shapiro, *The Hidden Cost of Being African American: How Wealth Perpetuates Inequality* (London: Oxford University Press, 2005); Michael Hout, "The Hidden Cost of Being African-American" (Review) in *The Washington Post*, 2005.

5. Robin D.G. Kelley, *Yo Mama's Dysfunktional! Fighting the Culture Wars in Urban America* (New York: Beacon Press, 1998), 77.

6. Bob Egelko, "5-4 decision disrupts schools' integration plans: Ruling condemns race-based enrollment and says districts must seek alternatives" in San Francisco Chronicle (June 29, 2007).

7. Cedric J. Robinson, *Black Movements in America* (New York: Routledge, 1997), 75.

8. George Lipsitz, "Abolition Democracy and Social Justice" in *Comparative American Studies: an International Journal* Volume 2, Number 3 (2004), 273.

9. Amaad Rivera, Brenda Cotto-Escalera, Anisha Desia, Jeaneatte Huezo, and Dedrick Muhammad, *Foreclosed: State of the Dream 2008* United For a Fair Economy, 2008.

10. Robin D.G. Kelley, *Freedom Dreams*, 9.

AMIRI BARAKA

Imagine Obama Talking to a Fool

To Lead, is what
We fought We fighting now, We been
At war
For equality, equal citizenship
Rights. Are those ours, No, no yet.
Our struggle Self Determination
Is always by the moment, is on us
Always, as our skin is, gleaming
Inside & outside w/ the fulfilled beauty
Of promise, as an eye arrow streaks
Through the darkness toward itself at
Thousands of miles an hour.
We are ourselves always
Full of ourselves. What we know
Is boundless as our everybody
All our hands & muscles, our swiftness
Is itself a thought & not a thought
But a being, a seeing, that, yes,
We want to lead, we are not fools
Or forever weaker than that self that cd
Be him, them, her, they, we can raise this
Stupid filthy place, we can strangle foolishness
Where it lurks and hurl it into hah hahs
Of imbecility. Why wd you taunt a person
With skeletons challenged by
The enlightenment?
So they turn the hood backwards
& now can see nothing
But how their weak breath
Makes the bedsheet soggy.
Yes, we can. Lead! We will anyway.

But we want to lead. What's wrong
With that? We can!
And with all this mountain pile
Of wrong, backward, dumb,
Dishonest, boring, filthy
Thing you or they have created
This thing that we us I have
Hated, It can not be a surprise
That someone else shd see this world
Through their own eyes. Yes,
I want to lead. You have
Already failed.
We have all hcard those songs
Those tales. I want to lead
You have already failed!

LaTasha Diggs

november 4th: elegua in satin

On election night
Harlem's rave party was heard in Brooklyn

a drum circle in Marcus Garvey park
cared less about an email suggesting a noose
be hung to jolt rooted fabrics

& next door
near Lenox, the State Building threw down till 3am
several house parties swarmed Edgecomb
& lord, drinks poured galore

we watched & many were quick
to diss the dress except me

no one recognized the flash of forcible nature
what it meant, how it adorned
the mounted
forgetful we, yes &   no,
the dress did not flatter much

but it was elegua I saw that night

the downpour splatter of scarlet
smeared over obsidian
her two girls matching her tactile esplanade
the boldness told me more than avatars
of fashion tribunals & fox news blusin'
to disarrange her
or even the flag flickering from her man's jacket

I told myself, watch when them necks are alert
something will churn in their guts,
howlin' with hunger. they'd prefer to garrote her. remember that.

three months later,
the Pequot's pickpocket salutes her
scoots over, & volunteers their pearly
praises her when she enters the Congressional domain
all unsullied subjects
all aged suspects of felons past & impending

now she's in purple.

44 ON **44**

Keep Living

More than three decades ago, I was working for *The Atlanta Constitution*, the morning newspaper in that city. My husband and I lived in an in-town neighborhood, so, most days, I traveled to and from work by bus and, if I worked late, returned home alone by cab.

Although the excitement of my job as an early black journalist on the staff of a mainstream morning daily newspaper, a career I had dreamed of, electrified me, the accommodations to my workday sometimes did not. The reporting was okay—getting the facts, interviewing city officials, community activists, visiting personalities. But what I truly savored was the writing of long thoughtful pieces on personalities or current trends or city living. Unfortunately, that writing often kept me at the newspaper offices downtown way into the night. And the prospect of jumping into the back seat of a taxicab in Atlanta or any city in those late hours left me filled with trepidation.

You see, I had a long history of clashes with city taxi drivers. They just did not seem to take to me. No matter how charming, polite and respectful I tried to be, no matter how substantial a tip I offered, no matter if I even accommodated their loud Christian music on the radio, they just did not cotton to me.

Even the father of a man I had been serious about gave me a disapproving look upon meeting me for the first time. You know I was on my best behavior. I couldn't understand his response until I learned his profession. He drove a cab for a living.

So late one night in the mid-1970s, when I hailed a taxi in front of the newspaper offices downtown to go home and jumped in the back seat, I assumed I was not in for a pleasant ride. However, when I announced my destination—754 Juniper Street—I was taken aback by the cab driver's response.

"Well, I'll be damned!" he uttered softly as he turned in his seat and looked at me up and down.

"Oh, great," I grumbled under my breath as I got myself, my purse and papers settled in the back seat. Another crazy cab driver who takes an instant disliking to me.

The black man at the wheel continued staring at me long past the time it felt seemly, even considering my history with taxicab drivers.

I sat squirming a bit in my seat for a while, considering the possibility of grabbing my purse and leaping from the parked taxi. Then the man turned and sat quietly for a moment more staring silently at the road ahead of him. Finally, he put the car in drive and took off slowly down Marietta Street.

Back then, there was no Plexiglas partition.

We rode in uneasy silence for a block or two. Then, the driver began to speak. At first, I thought he was talking to himself. But he looked up at me a few times in the rearview mirror, and when we made eye contact I realized that he was speaking to me.

"Years ago," he said, "there used to be this famous boxer. A black man named Tiger Flowers. He was a man who did a lot of talking and lots of folks just thought he was one of those people who was…well, crazy.

"Now, back then, didn't nothing but white folks live downtown in Atlanta in neighborhoods off Peachtree Street and around Piedmont Park. But Tiger, now he used to say all the time at barber shops and at restaurants and after his fights whenever black folks got together that one day there was gonna be black folks living in these houses downtown. In fact, he liked that building on Juniper Street; it was like a summer home to rich white people. And he would say in particular, some day, colored folks was going to be living in that very building.

"Well, you know, black folks then just laughed right in his face, even though he was a powerful built man, a boxer and all. The very idea that that would ever happen.

"But then, you get in my cab tonight and say, '754 Juniper Street.' And you live there. "Well…."

And his voice just trailed off. By that time, I realized that we were parked outside my three-story, U-shaped building on Juniper, and probably had been for some time. I hadn't noticed. I don't think I'd ever been quite as enthralled with a story before in my life.

Over the years, the decades really, I have never forgotten that experience and that cab driver's midnight story of wonder. And until

November of 2008, I don't believe I truly understood it. Oh, I had the facts.

For years, I researched Tiger Flowers. I've discovered that he was from Brunswick on the coast of Georgia, the area where I now live. That he was talented and gifted and bold and adventurous and more than a little bit crazy. He had foresight and forthrightness and vision. And he was not afraid to share that vision with just about anybody who came across his path.

During his time in Atlanta in the 1920s, he trained, became active in the local community and church and boxed his way to the top of his game as the number five all-time middleweight boxer, with a devastating left hand.

When he died during an operation in 1927, his manager was negotiating a re-match for the middleweight boxing championship of the world. And half a century later, he was still remembered by an African-American taxicab driver in Atlanta who had been one of the tens of thousands who had filed past Tiger Flowers' casket and paid their respects at his memorial service at the old Atlanta City Auditorium.

As I sat with my husband in our home on the Georgia coast, and with just about all the rest of America and the world riveted to the final tallies of the 2008 presidential elections, I couldn't help but think of that amazed cab driver in Atlanta back in 1977 and of Tiger Flowers back in the same city in the 1920s.

"Well, I'll be damned," I muttered to myself as I sat in front of the television screen as it seemed certain that there was about to be a sea change in this country, which a little over a century before had bought and sold and enslaved human beings—my ancestors. A country which a bit more than half a century ago had denied all its citizens the right to live where and how they wished and according to what they could afford. A country which even in my parents' day could hardly envision a time when their daughter would be able to graduate from college and compete on a fairer playing field with other white fledgling journalists for top jobs in their field. That that same country would band together enough to elect a person of color for the highest office in the land was enough to leave the world shaking its collective heads.

I had to laugh at myself, the way that Tiger Flowers or even Barack Obama may have chuckled at me and my wonder of the moment.

I'm not comparing Tiger Flowers to President Barack Obama, a man of color and vision who, too, had the nerve, smarts and stamina to tackle an overarching challenge. But that association is not really too much of a stretch.

Men, people of vision are often quite similar.

In the late summer of 2007 at the national meeting of the National Association of Black Journalists in Las Vegas, I sat in a huge auditorium surrounded by African-American journalists trying their best to be impartial and objective as presidential candidate Obama took the stage for a brief statement and then a Q & A.

When asked what his election would mean, Obama replied in a way that spoke to the hearts and experiences of just about everyone in that auditorium. He said the deepest effect would be in how it would change the American psyche, white people and black people, to see his two girls running and playing on the south lawn of the White House. This picture of Sasha and Malia against the backdrop of the White House, their father said, would humanize the image of black children, black families, black people everywhere in a way that had never happened before. And, he added, it would not only affect white people in this country and the world. More importantly, it would also change the view of ourselves to ourselves.

A little more than a year later, I witnessed just what our 44th president predicted as he, his wife and his girls took to the stage in Chicago on the night of the election. The crowds cheered. The country wept, and our hearts swelled with emotion. And I witnessed the same when the First Family moved into 1600 Pennsylvania Avenue weeks later.

Tiger Flowers was right. One day black folks would be occupying houses, places, offices, jobs, levels that even many black folks could not envision. An African-American woman jumping into a cab at midnight in front of a big city newspaper office was just the beginning. As Tiger Flowers might have said, "Keep Living."

KELLY NORMAN ELLIS

Crossing Over: Invocation for the New Flag
(November 4, 2008)

This is a new song
for the crossing over.
new anthem,
new banner
to be waved.
here is the new flag embroidered
with Choctaw sassafras root
with Harlem, the Delta, Washington Heights
and every Chinatown everywhere,
the Nigerian girl braiding hair in Chi,
the Eritrean driving a cab in Philly.
this is a flag for the creole of Treme,
the bursting murals of Pilsen
the wings of flying Tuskegee men.

wave this flag like it was never a lie
for those who pray five times a day,
for Bessie Smith's Affrilachian Mountain,
for the American Issei and Nisei,
for Chaney, Goodman and Sherwner,
for Malcolm in his winding sheet
and all the *Native Sons*
Bigger and Medgar and Baldwin and Alexie
for Harvey Milk
and all the ones who can't because
we won't.

for the ones who chanted
Today's a good day to die
for Leonard Peltier and Wilma Mankiller,
for Robeson and Einstein,

the hustler on the El
and the banger on my corner.
for Ethel Rosenberg in the electric chair.
I am crossing over now
for all Zora's Yoruba Seminole songs,
for Vietnamese shrimpers in Galveston
and Sacagawea and Studs Turkel and
for Denise, Carole, Addie Mae and Cynthia of
Birmingham,
John Reed and Harold Washington,
DuBois and Booker,
Martin, Rosa and Fannie Lou,
for Pete Seeger, Marvin Gaye,
Coltrane, Nina Simone
and all the See Line Women.
this is the crossing over banner
about the Sioux and Chickasaw and Choctaws and
the Hopi and Iroquois and Cherokee,
for all the Husseins and Fatimas,
for Jesus and Esparanza,
for those who sat in
and those who cut down
the lyncher's nooses.
for Matthew Shepard and Ida B.

for Barack and Michelle and Malia and Sasha
opening themselves like soft black wings.
I will fashion a new flag
from the old one folded like a triangle
and buried
in my black grandfather's Mississippi
grave.

NATASHA TRETHEWEY

Another Country

A few years ago, when I was working on the poem, "My Mother Dreams Another Country," I was compelled to consider what my mother must have been thinking—in 1966—about the biracial child she and my father were bringing into the world. The year before, my parents had broken two laws of the state of Mississippi by traveling to Ohio to marry and then returning to my mother's home state. It was just after the passage of the 1964 Civil Rights Act and the 1965 Voting Rights Act, but still before the Supreme Court decision in *Loving v. State of Virginia* in which state anti-miscegenation laws were ruled unconstitutional. And it was years before those unconstitutional state laws were no longer enforced—by custom, by intimidation, and by other deterrents imposed upon couples seeking marriage licenses. Barack Obama was just 5 years old when my mother was contemplating another country—another America—in which interracial marriage would be legal in the entire country. In 1961, when Obama was born, 21 states still had laws forbidding the marriage of his parents—of blacks to whites.

The vestiges of those old laws still hang on in the customs and attitudes of many people in the United States. In Alabama, for example, it has been just about a decade since citizens went to the polls to vote on whether or not the anti-miscegenation law should be removed from the books. The old law was voted down by a slim margin. Nearly half of the people casting their ballots wanted to keep the law—if only symbolically, —in order to support the antiquated notion that parents like mine shouldn't be able to marry legally in the state, and—by extension—people like me, and Obama, be legally born.

Perhaps my mother, contemplating the shifting language and mores of her time, imagined the kind of psychological exile I would inherit as a native daughter of a state and a country that rendered me symbolically illegal—an imposed "illegitimacy" underscored by the laws of the land. Perhaps, also, she worried—as any concerned parent would—about the kind of nation her child would inherit in which people of color, poor people, and other marginal citizens continued to be pushed to the periphery of American citizenship—a liminal space, a country within a country, in which social justice, equal protection under the law, and equal opportunity in education, housing and health care were dreams we are as yet working as a nation to ensure for all American citizens.

Watching the election of Barack Obama to become the 44th president of the United States —(the first black person and first biracial person to hold this office)—I couldn't help thinking of my mother, dead 23 years now. Were she here to witness this moment in American history, she might recall, as I do, lines from Langston Hughes' famous poem "I, Too, Sing America." She would no doubt take note of just how far we have come as a nation, reveling in the symbolic imagery of an American citizen stepping from the margins of our shared history to lead us in the continued pursuit of liberty and justice for all.

She'd also have a sober assessment of how much we have left to do.

* * *

My Mother Dreams Another Country

Already the words are changing. She is changing
     from *colored* to *negro*, *black* still years ahead.
This is 1966—she is married to a white man—
     and there are more names for what grows inside her.
It is enough to worry about words like *mongrel*
     and the infertility of mules and *mulattoes*
while flipping through a book of baby names.
     She has come home to wait out the long months,
her room unchanged since she's been gone:
     dolls winking down from every shelf—all of them
white. Every day she is flanked by the rituals of superstition,
     and there is a name she will learn for this too:
maternal impression—the shape, like an unknown
     country, marking the back of the newborn's thigh.
For now, women tell her to clear her head, to steady her hands

or she'll gray a lock of the child's hair wherever
she worries her own, imprint somewhere the outline
        of a thing she craves too much. They tell her
to stanch her cravings by eating dirt. All spring
        she has sat on her hands, her fingers numb. For awhile
each day, she can't feel anything she touches: the arbor
        out back—the landscape's green tangle; the molehill
of her own swelling. Here—outside the city limits—
        cars speed by, clouds of red dust in their wake.
She breathes it in—*Mississippi*—then drifts toward sleep,
        thinking of someplace she's never been. Late,
Mississippi is a dark backdrop bearing down
        on the windows of her room. On the TV in the corner,
the station signs off, broadcasting its nightly salutation:
        the waving stars and stripes, our national anthem.

Bridge from MLK, Jr. to BHO, Jr.: Span of a Lifetime

I've been ruminating about this article for two months. Now I'm down to the wire and forced to sit down to begin writing. The problem is not procrastination, as much as it is the *weight* of this span of time from August 28, 1963, the March on Washington to August 28, 2008, the day Barack Hussein Obama was nominated as the Democratic Party standard-bearer for the Presidency of the United States of America. Actually, the span is best seen looking backward from the Inauguration of President Barack Obama on January 20, 2009, because the occasion took me back to the grounds of the Washington Mall where I watched Dr. Martin Luther King, Jr. deliver his spellbinding speech, "I Have a Dream."

I fear also that looking back over that span might be too autobiographical and bore people to tears. But it is what I have to offer. It is the most compelling experience for me, as I reflect on the election of the 44th President of the United States. The two occasions stand as bookends to an exciting and fortunate life I have lived, about which I am often encouraged to write as a book. So perhaps this article will act as a test drive for a larger work.

Most profound about this arch of history is my opportunity to play a role in the historic period between the two bookends. I heard a preacher at a funeral say that "although the deceased's life span printed on the funeral program says '1930-2008,' neither of those dates mean as much as the dash in the middle. It is in that dash, that a person lives his life." It is in the dash between Martin Luther King, Jr. and Barack Hussein Obama, Jr. that I have been fortunate, not to just be an observer, but to have played a role, albeit a small role.

Much of the joy of Obama's inauguration in Washington, DC, came from the work we did in the campaign with the African Americans for Obama in Pittsburgh, which I established in November 2007 in anticipation of the upcoming Pennsylvania Primary. The Clinton-Obama showdown in Pennsylvania had all the dramatic buildup of the Thrilla in Manila. While Clinton and Obama fought in other states for their 8, 10 or 12 delegates, Pennsylvania had a grand prize of 22 delegates. The Governor Ed Rendell had lined up the entire apparatus of the state Democratic Party for Hillary Clinton—all the elected officials from statewide officials down to local school boards; the state Democratic Party Chairman, all the county party chairs, as well as the precinct committee officials. They were fired up for Hillary!

We even had to suffer the humiliation of the black woman who won my City Council seat, stumping for Hillary, while the overwhelming majority of the voters in the district were strong for Obama. She said that she was supporting Hillary because she didn't want to waste her vote; she wanted to pick a winner! She reminded us of Gov. Sarah Palin, who sneered about Obama, "What is a Community Organizer anyway?" She sneered and she snickered until the Community Organizing train ran her over. She doesn't ask, "What is a Community Organizer?" anymore. Painfully, she now knows! They all know.

On the other side of the road–on the far left–we had a chorus line of a different kind, with super-black activists suggesting that supporting Obama was not much different than supporting any other Democrat. This far left blabber actually took them out of the election altogether, even though they claimed to represent the black masses, who were overwhelmingly supportive of Obama. So were they leading those masses, or tailing them?

On a national level, Tavis Smiley spawned a lot of this talk after Obama offered to send his wife Michelle to the Smiley confab in New Orleans, as he was a little busy getting himself elected to the Presidency. Smiley declined the offer (what is Michelle Obama, chopped liver?) and then went around the country bad-mouthing Obama. So while Tavis and his Smiley's were busy bad-mouthing Obama, black "leftists" missed a huge opportunity to position themselves to actually influence the Obama campaign in a way that could have moved the national debate forward and reap benefits for the black masses they claimed to be representing.

It was a breath of fresh air to finally receive a copy of a paper written by Amiri Baraka, putting the presidential election in perspective and laying out a progressive agenda for anyone who wanted to really make a difference in the election, or in the country, for that matter.

Hillary beat us pretty bad in the Pennsylvania Primary, so the victory of delivering Pennsylvania for Obama in the General Election was especially sweet. At the end of the day on Election Day, I invited all the Obama volunteers who worked in my neighborhood to our family neighborhood bar, the Red Onion East, to watch the returns. The moment slowly heated up as the early returns came in on CNN. There was a loud cheer when Wolf Blitzer announced that Obama had indeed won Pennsylvania, and that no Republican had ever won the White House without winning Pennsylvania. But still, the West Coast polling places had not yet closed. The jury was still out. The bar was getting jam-packed. The major local TV news station had decided to camp out at the Red Onion East to catch the reaction of the crowd when the winner was announced.

Finally, at 11 PM EST, Wolf Blitzer, in one, extended sentence announced, "The polls on the West Coast have closed and CNN projects California to go to Barack Obama and CNN is now able to report that Barack Obama will be the next President of the United States of America." DA JOINT WENT WILD. Screaming. Jumping. Hugging. Crying. You would have thought it was Juneteenth, 1865! What a moment.

I thought about that Red Onion moment when Obama placed his hand on Lincoln's bible to be sworn in. I looked at the mass of humanity assembled for the occasion. I had never seen this many people gathered in the same place; as it was in 1963 at the young age of twenty, I had never seen that many people gathered in the same place.

Dr. King's dream inspired me to join-up as a Freedom Rider, when I was supposed to go to the Mississippi Delta for four summer months of 1965, then return to college to learn how to become a Negro businessman. Four months turned into four years. I never got back to college. Instead, I was educated by the stern hand of the Mississippi Ku Klux Klan! The King-inspired journey to the Mississippi Delta was actually the beginning of a long journey that would take me through years of organizing against legal segregation, through the Black Power coup of the Student Nonviolent Coordinating Committee (SNCC), through the rise of black nationalism and the formation of the Congress of African People (CAP).

Back in Pittsburgh, we put those community organizing skills to work, creating institutions that have lasted to this very day, such as the Africana Studies Program and the student-led Black Action Society at the University of Pittsburgh; the Black Horizons Theatre, replaced by Kuntu Repertory Theater, which produced work by Rob Penny and Pulitzer Prize winner August Wilson; the House of the Crossroads Drug Rehabilitation Program; and the Western PA Black Political Assembly, which led to the election of a succession of progressive political representatives, including the eventual 1995 election of this writer to the Pittsburgh City Council, where I served for 11 years.

It is a similar legacy such as this, in cities all across the nation, where alumni of the civil rights movement, the black nationalist movement, the anti-Viet Nam war movement and CAP, and others laid the groundwork for the eventual arrival of another community organizer from Chicago to roll across this country like a Sherman Tank, running over a squeaky-voiced governor asking, "What is a community organizer anyway?" on his way to 1600 Pennsylvania Avenue, Washington, D.C.

Well, now he's there. What do we do now? He said throughout the campaign, "This isn't about me. I can't do this by myself. This is about you–the people." Unfortunately, the progressive black community did not organize, so as to position itself to take good advantage of this moment. We are organizationally, geographically and ideologically dispersed all across the land. Other constituency groups are already in the White House, shaping and advancing their agenda. It will take us a little while longer, I suppose.

But this is an opportunity that will not come back around for a long time. Four years will pass very quickly. Eight years will pass even more quickly. The time to cull together a progressive, national political agenda is now.

GoBama!!!

EUGENE B. REDMOND

Passing the Baton: From King to President

Prologue

(This is a drama designed for Shakespeare,
Lorraine Hansberry or August Wilson:
A muscular, secular messiah,
thin as a Masai warrior,
ascends the Inaugural Stage—
struttin' like a bop-royal cat daddy
in a Duke Ellington "Caravan"—
just four & a half decades
after the dream-king placed a
freedom ring [ring-ring] on America's altar.)

First Kwansaba

gone—sit beside your self home boy—
while the dalai lama does a samba,
& four tops strut ole georgia slop,
morton's belly rolls its jelly—with nelly—&
dunham's meringue matches haiti's shay shay. then
honolulu's juju hails chicago's choo-choo as
it hauls dues outta east saint blues

I.

The warrior is a hum of hope
in a skin-splitting winter of economic horror,
while proud old schoolers back-flash,
remembering when, as civil souljahs,
we car- , train- , foot- , bus- & love-pooled
from East Saint Louis—

shepherded by Elmo J. Bush & Clyde C. Jordan,
Homer G. Randolph & Ethele Scott—
to a then-New Day's Door in D.C.
—August, nineteen sixty-three—
to hear a martyr-to-be named Martin.

Second Kwansaba

how's 2-morrow gonna anoint you—o
rail-slim, genius-phat—home joy? maybe
"prez" like jazz peers hailed lester young?
perhaps with soulos on blues-phonic hearts
muted & stroked by miles-cool fingers?
in rhyme, mime or Kenya—sublime? maybe
a combo: kansas wiz & chicago gusto?

II.

Who knew we'd return in two-thousand-nine—
a rainbow of nations, globes & galaxies—
to the chocolate city,
some whirling along ghostly ancestrails,
offering hallelujahs & hails
to a chocolate First Family,
steppin' thru door Forty-Four
of a vanilla-colored prize
bathed in four-hundred-year-old eyes?

Who knew we'd be makers of kings & prezes?

That atop this mountain of history's
many-many beginnings,
including its cradling of movements & martyrs,
we would shuttle from thrones to chains
to shackles to chattel to thrones?

That over centuries, vigil drummers of justice
would record racial progression & regression
like Benjamin Banneker surveyed Washington
in the late seventeen hundreds?

That song-bred continuums—field hollas
& street anthems, Paul Robesons & Leon Thomases,
Fisk Jubilee Singers & Wings Over Jordan,
Mahalias & Arethas, Muddy Waters
& warbling William Warfields—would assemble
their choral power at this Inaugural Hour?

Kwansaba Encore

hand-to-hand love craft steada combat,
we chuck walk/swivel plural minds to
berry's, stevie's & springsteen's wonder-rolls—oral
scrolls—echoing yet more hollas & "steal-
always," drummin' rivers, hookin' arms, sharin' alms
& psalms of handed-down shoes bearin'
gabriel-good news . . . "Yes, Kindred, We Did!"

That a dream, snipered in Memphis in sixty-eight,
would re-arrive, alive—out of barrels of hate—
      —as freedom incarnate—
    a baton passed from King to President?

January 20, 2009/July 9, 2009

KEITH GILYARD

From King to Obama

Of the feverish attempts to define the essence of Barack Obama's triumphant bid for the presidency, the strongest contender for dominant narrative is that his victory fulfilled the dream of Martin Luther King, Jr. Millions of tee shirts promote this conception as fact. King-Obama posters grace the walls of African-American living rooms, modernizing and, in many instances, replacing the displays that long featured King, John Kennedy, and Robert Kennedy in separate frames. Indeed, consolidated King-Obama images have probably already outsold the iconic photographs of King and Malcolm X shaking hands in the halls of the U.S. Senate on March 26, 1964. In the main library at the Pennsylvania State University in University Park, an imposing exhibit features the phrase "his dream" below a likeness of King; the wordage "our reality" beneath a depiction of Obama. The alpha chronicle is gobbling up institutions.

None need deny that Obama's riveting ascension to the White House enacts *one* of King's dreams, as King did speak of a time when the nation's chief executive would be African American. Nor should anyone downplay the monumental racial achievement Obama's story is. The inauguration multitudes spoke loudly enough. Nonetheless, all tales should be scrutinized lest they become dangerously hegemonic. Therefore, it is crucial that fuller versions of King's vision, given he was as important a prophet as we had in the latter half of the twentieth century, be kept before the twenty-first-century public to enable adequate analysis. At the same time, it is useful to examine some of the related commonplaces circulating, most notably, that we saw assessment of qualifications prevail over judgment of melanin and are now entering a post-racial political era in America.

Only a loose interpretation of King's words as expressed at the March on Washington could suggest the wishes he expressed on that occasion have been satisfactorily implemented. There still exists an oversupply of segregation manacles, discrimination chains, and bad checks. As for interfaith hand holding, much of white America could not even accept Obama the black Christian joining hands with Reverend Jeremiah Wright, the prophetic and righteously indignant black Christian preacher who had sermonized to him for twenty years. Moreover, we witnessed how the mere charge of "Muslim" severely damaged the Obama candidacy in some quarters. And concerning relatively progressive politics, Obama failed to carry the red hills of Georgia, the molehills of Mississippi, or much of the territory around Lookout Mountain in Tennessee.

Perhaps the most remarked upon aspect of King's most famous address is his articulated desire that his four little children would be judged as adults not by the color of their skin, but by the content of their character. His children were a metaphor for the likes of Obama. One, Dexter, was born the same year as the president. But we have little tangible evidence that Obama clinched his job because of character. For one, we don't know what his character is. We'll find out over the course of the next four to eight years when we observe him under enough stress and pressure, enough complexity and dilemma, enough of the situations that reveal one's fundamental substance. Is he the undercover radical some suppose? That's a very doubtful proposition, though he refreshingly leans well left of Limbaugh logic. Has he really had some Tony Rezko-style wheeler-dealer in him? Probably, somewhat given, that any politician emerging from rough and tumble Chicago has almost unavoidably been beholden to some special interest. What we know for sure is we have elected a chief executive of supercharged ambition, impressive intellect, rhetorical brilliance, incredible charisma, admirable energy, and unmistakable cool. Down the line we'll see about issues of character, say, integrity and resolve, qualities put under tremendous strain by politics.

But if Obama's victory was not the literal achievement of the ideas King spoke about at the March on Washington, a symbolic Martin Luther King, Jr., the one in the minds of many Obama supporters, nonetheless paved much of the way and powered the effort. *That* King was invaluable and irreplaceable. However, we should not lose touch with the real one who, in the years following the March on Washington, elaborated on his basic political impulses, although those latter pronouncements are usually not what people have in mind when they speak of King's dream—not at Obama campaign time or on any January 15th.

In his last book, *Where Do We Go from Here: Chaos or*

Community?, King claimed that deep structural changes in the American political and economic system were required if social justice, essentially meaning the elimination of poverty nationally and internationally, were to be realized. He called for a guaranteed income pegged to median income, championed the reform of housing markets, and outlined plans for revamping public education. The pressure to force such changes would, in his view, be applied by a powerful multiethnic coalition of liberals, labor activists, and civil rights proponents, all united by the goal of "Power for Poor People." The white poor, therefore, were important to King's vision of a peaceful and prosperous world house. Obama didn't fare too well with the white poor, or at least not the white working class, which opted for McCain over him 58 percent to 40 percent. Of course, poor people of color went overwhelmingly for Obama. King, a one-time Republican, would have been dismayed to see that the white working class thought the present Republican Party represented their best choice.

The white working class pretty much shaped the white voting response overall. Although 61 percent of those who voted for Obama were white, John McCain outpolled him among white voters 55 percent to 43 percent. Obama won two percent more of the white vote than Kerry did in 2004, but less than the 47 percent Jimmy Carter garnered in 1976. Another way of framing the numbers is this: If only the white electorate, which is 74 percent of the total electorate, voted, McCain would have won easily. He won the white South, where the least organized white working class has long resided, 68 percent to 32 percent.

Obama rode the African and Hispanic vote to the winner's circle. African Americans, 13 percent percent of the American electorate, delivered 95 percent of their vote to Obama. Hispanics, 9 percent of the voters, contributed 67 percent of their vote to Obama, the best showing among Hispanics by a Democratic presidential candidate in the nation's history. All the talk suggesting Hispanics would not support a black candidate proved inconsequential, as Gabriel Sanchez, a University of New Mexico political science professor, correctly predicted. Asian Americans, about 4 percent percent of the electorate, didn't swing any state—Hispanics swung Indiana—but they loom, because of their concentration in key states like California, as an important swing vote in future elections.

This all suggests not a post-racializing of America, but a re-racializing of America. Or, cast another way, we are seeing a new spin inside an extended racial period. The new math for candidates is clear, and the party foisting Bobby Jindal and Michael Steele on you knows it. Even if one takes 55 percent of the white vote—it's difficult to take much more—he has to do moderately well among constituencies of color. Five percent of the African American vote and 33 percent of the Hispanic vote will not secure you victory. Conversely, if one you can attract 95 percent of the African American vote and 67 percent of the Hispanic ballots, strategically distributed, you can concede 57 percent percent of the white vote and make it to the White House.

The new math indicates that more national triumphs may be in the offing for candidates of color. The white percentage of the electorate is shrinking; the most racially diverse demographic are voters under thirty, the only age group in which more white votes went to Obama than to McCain. But no run will be easy. Obama has often termed his campaign improbable, and he is correct in more ways than he has discussed publicly. He had to demonstrate he was black enough but not too black, surprise in Iowa, stagger under the weight of the teary-eyes-technique in New Hampshire, regain momentum in South Carolina courtesy of bumbling Clintonian calculations about African American sensibility, overcome the surge of Sarah Palin's mindless "kill Obama" minions, reap the benefits of McCain's dismal response to the financial sector's collapse, and survive the defection of 17 percent of the Hillary Democrats. For succeeding, the prize is a mountain of trouble. King would not have figured things would be any easier.

A re-racialized America can install an exceptional candidate of color, but not yet dispatch poverty—a condition one third of all black children live in—or dispense with institutional racism. The typical white family possesses a net worth eleven times that of the average African American family and eight times that of the average Hispanic family. Much of this disparity results from discrimination in real estate practices. For example, by some estimates, African Americans have lost 500 billion dollars of wealth because of historical housing discrimination. They are turned down by prime lenders, denied fixed-rate mortgages they can afford, are steered by those lenders to affiliated business predators for adjustable-rate mortgages, which are hard to pay, especially given that, even prior to the current financial disaster, blacks lost an estimated 120 billion dollars annually because of discrimination in labor markets. Then the victims are called greedy and fiscally irresponsible because they danced with the sub-prime lenders. But just because one is guilty of dancing with the devil, it doesn't mean it's not the devil.

Matters like these are what a liberal reformer of any color needs to address in a movement toward what King described as a "socially conscious democracy which reconciles the truths of individualism and collectivism." In Obama, we may indeed have that much-postulated transformational figure. And what he accomplishes with the practical powers of his office may not be his greatest legacy. Inspiring new waves of young people to choose lives of progressive political commitment, lives conducted within cross-ethnic and multiethnic alliances and, as King phrased it, on the high plane of dignity and discipline, could be his greatest contribution.

The youth vote did not put Obama in the White House. If no one under the age of thirty voted, only Indiana and North Carolina, among the states he carried, would have gone in the Republican column. But youth, particularly Millennials, were certainly catalytic in terms of getting voters of all ages to the polls. If these Millennials stay energized, as they must to bring greater social justice to America, that is a story King would be most proud to write.

Jericho Brown

Receiving Line

California, November 2008

Whenever a man wins, other men form lines
To wring his right hand like a towel wet
With what anyone wants after washing. None

Of us clean, we leave a soot older than color
Caked in his palm, so the winner we waited for
Can't see his own lifeline. This is mine,

Suited, on time: *My name is Jericho Brown.*
I like a little blues and a lot of whiskey. I read
When my children let me. I write what I can't

Resist. I'm as proud of you as a well-built chest, and
I am in unlegislated love with a man bound
To grab for me when he sleeps. Take my right hand,

The one that wakes him, the one I use to swear—
What more must men hold in common if seized
By grips as firm as history, as stiff as risk.

President Obama and Organizing

The fact that the USA has an African American president is an eventuality that began long before he or I was born. This reality was bathed in the blood, tears, sweat and toil of untold masses of our people and others, in the historical struggle against slavery, for human rights and the power to control our own destiny. President Barack Hussein Obama's campaign, election victory and inauguration were and are yet another step in the people's struggle to advance the cause for democracy and self-determination.

As one of a number of young activists trying to change America in the 60s, I'd learned from Maulana Karenga (US organization), Amiri Baraka and CAP (Congress of African Peoples) that there were "four ends to political power, i.e., *political office*; community organization; alliances and coalitions; and disruption, threatened or actual." This lesson was a major part of what we learned and knew and what we were taught over and over during those days. Now, 40 years since I was so enlightened with these gems of political wisdom, I was again using this teaching as a practical, workable tool and approach to my work in the Obama Campaign for Change. Organizing around electoral politics gives some activists cause for concern, but other revolutionaries throughout history seemed to have grasped and employed this concept to their advantage.

"The little skinny guy with the strange name," Barack describing himself struck a chord with me, because it sounded so much like CAP. We were an entire organization of little skinny guys and girls with strange names, working in inner-city communities across the US, many of whom had long since abandoned the notions of middle class comfort and aspirations for the rigors of grassroots community organizing and black nation building.

Upon my return to Cleveland in the mid 70s, I was being touted as a possible candidate for public office for a city council seat. I recall fellow activists and potential campaign workers wondering and strategizing, like Obama once did, on how we would deal with my African name issue. Thus, we went on and on brainstorming; community organizers, activists and revolutionaries trying to strategize a move to political power. Needless to say, that campaign never materialized, however, after that experience, Barack's dilemma seemed all too familiar. I felt I knew exactly what he was facing, so getting involved with his campaign was easy but not automatic. I had worked in both of Jessie Jackson's campaigns and came away with a lot of good experiences but also with some trepidation. The view that our energy, our work and integrity had been betrayed was one such feeling. It is easy to get cynical after such episodes.

I recalled all the obstacles that were placed in Jessie's path. "He had never held public office," "he doesn't have experience" and the like were hurled ad nauseam by the American media, bigots and others to deny this contemporary run for national public office. I remembered thinking that it was all a sham, a bogus argument, but I also reasoned that if we took those arguments away from the naysayers, what new bullshit would they invent to stifle black political empowerment? After Jessie, I knew that the same arguments would doom Sharpton's campaign essentially before it could begin, but both campaigns at a minimum kept the notion of an African American holding national office in the mind of blacks and the nation. Jessie had in fact run a memorable campaign in 1984, meaning, he was the better prepared candidate ideologically, so much so, that I put aside years of misgivings about him to work in his campaign. I was with a national labor union by then and coordinated the vast resources that labor can bring to bear on a national campaign.

Now in observing Senator Obama's run for the White House, in its earliest days, I was intrigued by the fact that his candidacy had answers to the arguments that the pundits and naysayers would put forth to try and derail his run, but, true to form, they ushered out many of the same old worn arguments, "not enough experience," "hadn't done anything major in his life," etc. One thing that they couldn't use, that they had used to hobble Jessie and Al's chances was the "never held public office" argument. "You can't use that here, so now what?" I asked. Another thing that I noticed when I went to Obama's public rally on Georgia Tech's campus rather early in his campaign, was that he had garnered the attention of numerous young people of all races and ethnicities—black, white, Asian, and Latino.

I called Amiri Baraka, concerned about the lack of black national leadership saying anything about Obama's campaign. Amiri said he had written a couple of articles that he would send to me. I went online and found an audio clip of a speech Amiri had given in New York regarding the campaign. I also received Amiri's article via email. In his article, Amiri was trying to articulate to the black left the importance of supporting Obama and or participating in electoral politics. As always, Amiri was dead on point. His writings, for me, always seem to open up a world of clarity, and he invariably has a way with words that puts a lot of the bullshit in check. He checked the folks that were saying Obama wasn't black enough, and he checked the folks saying that electoral politics was bourgeois politics. I wondered though, why was Amiri spending his time meeting and debating with the so called black left, who in many instances seemed still trapped in the notion of endless theoretical discussions as a substitute for practical work?

As an organizer, it always seemed to me that the movement would be better served drawing upon the millions of new folks that appeared eager to get involved and who were not ideologically jaded nor suffering from a certain amount of ideological paralysis as some of our veteran brothers and sisters. I guess we owe them some deference, but I have never thought that a movement began with trying to organize the so-called organized. My own experience had shown that a good organizer can go on any campus or in any community and mobilize, organize and rally folks to act on issues that concern them. And if the organizer shows patience and commitment, these new recruits will often not just act for a semester or a meeting, but for a sustained period of time.

Obama's campaign harnessed that same type of momentum. It hadn't necessarily sought approval from all of the old heads of the movement; it drew in millions of community folks and young first-time activists on the foot soldier level. I recalled meeting a white woman who had worked with Obama's effort in South Carolina and was now in Georgia, packing up to head to the next primary states. She was not a paid staffer; she was a volunteer no less, a person who wanted to see change in the US. Obama's campaign was accomplishing a certain coalescence of various nationalities around the promise for change, not revolution mind you, but just the promise for change. That reality was good enough for me, all revolutions have to start somewhere and ideologically, I reasoned that this national movement for political office by an African American candidate had a certain amount of promise in that a lot of fresh blood was being rallied and that by being involved, I would get a practical feel as to where people were politically. In my opinion, this was an excellently organized movement and I couldn't understand why folks would want to sit on the sidelines. I believed the motion surrounding the campaign was deep enough that activists should get involved to give it additional relevance. After all, here was a candidate who continually urged "this is not about me, it is about you," "you are the one, that we have been waiting for," and that message seemed very clear to me.

I wanted to get in this motion, but not in any official campaign office capacity. I wanted in as a grassroots organizer, putting into practice once again the techniques that had been learned in Newark, Pittsburgh, Cleveland, Detroit, Wrightsville and so many other places over the past forty years.

During the Super Tuesday Primary in Atlanta, I commandeered a 6'x4' Obama sign from campaign headquarters and positioned myself on an Island at an exit ramp off of Interstate 285. I extolled motorists to vote and blow their horns to show support. I saw firsthand that Obama's campaign had captured the hopes and imagination of the masses. That intersection was animated with motorists blowing their horns and waving their fists in the air.

After the Georgia and South Carolina primaries, I headed to Mississippi, staying with my brother in Columbus, Mississippi. There, I immediately began to take stock of the physical resources I would have access to. I spoke with friends of my brother and others. I was introduced to an old white chicken farmer, who upon introduction, immediately began to explain that he had never been racist, that he had lived through hard times just like the blacks had. Many of his assertions couldn't be verified, but here in Mississippi, this unsolicited confessional was at least encouraging for the work ahead of me.

The following morning my brother and I headed to Clarksdale, the place where I was born, and had not returned to since my mother relocated her family to Cleveland, Ohio after the brutal lynching of Emmitt Till. The lynching took place some forty or so miles down the road from where we played as children. Now I was back there, trying to get the first black president elected in the US.

A multitude of thoughts raced through my mind about this place, for it was there that the acute and pernicious rampage of segregation and Jim Crow was so thorough, that it left many black youth either dead or psychologically crippled. It was there that I saw the savage nature of racism up close as a child—a black man burned to death in his car less than thirty yards from our front door, another black man mowed down by Mississippi sheriffs, police and assorted racist vigilantes at the cotton mill at the end of the alley where we lived. This was my reality as a child, so what do you mean a black president is meaningless?

Wanda, an Obama fieldworker, had driven down from Indiana and was staying at a local hotel in Clarksdale. My cousin Virdel drove me over to meet with her and she supplied us with what literature she had. We leafleted at a Walmart and in black communities throughout Clarksdale. This place looked so different than what I remembered as a child. I had never realized as a child that our house was in an alley, and that Mr. Sugar's juke joint was on the corner of that alley.

We left Clarksdale trying to get back to Columbus in time to catch Obama at a local university, but we missed that event. I was able to get some local residents to help me leaflet a Walmart parking lot. I will never forget the elderly black women I came upon in that lot talking to each other about Obama. They had been to the rally and they were talking excitedly about his chances of winning and that they certainly hoped he would be able to do what he said he would do, should he win. One remarked to the other, rather adoringly, "He is such a good looking man, too." At that precise moment they noticed me and began to laugh, knowing I had overheard their conversation. They took the flyers and kept laughing and smiling as I walked away. In that same parking lot, one of the recruits on the leafleting detail encountered a white woman that took the flyer and tore it up and threw it to the ground. This individual was lucky that we were on a bigger mission. Some things in Mississippi may never change.

I drove from Mississippi back to Georgia in preparation for my journey north to Gary, Indiana, where in 1972, an activist named Kasisi Nakawa and I carried out the final preparation for the arrival of delegates to what would become the historic Gary Black Political Convention and the establishment of the National Black Political Assembly. This convention was so important then and was another one of the historical foundations for Obama's current campaign. So much national organizing went into the Gary convention. I had worked with Naisha, Kiburi, Sanjulo, Masai, Tukufu, Sala and others, traveling all over Eastern Pennsylvania to the Ohio line to organize for the Allegheny County Black Political Convention. Ron Daniels from Youngstown had come over to Pittsburgh to observe, and would go on to be instrumental in convening the Ohio Black Political Convention. This same type of work was occurring across the country. Gary brought back a slew of memories and it afforded me an opportunity to see my daughter and grandson, residing there. I signed on with the local Obama office, working with Trey Daniels (a young Hampton graduate) and others. A local Gary resident named Cleo and I became a formidable team, we erected large signs on thoroughfarcs, distributed yards signs, ran sound cars, did phone calls and door to door canvassing. It was like old times in Gary. I remembered 1972, when Vice Mayor Jessie Bell gave up his office in city hall to Nakawa and me, to do convention work. This was what having political power meant when done right, access to resources so as to be able deliver the goods and services to the people. Without the support of Mayor Hatcher's administration, the Gary convention would have been difficult if not impossible. In 2008, at the close of the Indiana primary, Barack Obama lost the State by a mere 14,000 votes, winning 34 delegates to Hillary Clinton's 38.

I left Gary and headed back South contacting friends in upcoming primary states; Ben Yusuf in Ohio kept in almost daily contact. I reached out to Sala and Marini in Pittsburgh, Pennsylvania. The primaries were heading toward completion with big fights remaining in those two states. Obama's North Carolina win and close call in Indiana had restored the campaign's momentum. However, the primaries would drag on to the bitter end, and contrary to what the national media would have you believe, the masses were following this as if it was an Ali-Frazier fight. They were keenly aware of racism being introduced into the race and were already inquiring about alternatives if the powers that be stole or attempted to steal the election from the obvious winner. This is not conjecture; this is where the masses were/are regarding their political consciousness.

With all primaries over, Obama was finally declared the winner. For the General Election fight, I elected to stay and work in Georgia. My involvement would be total, i.e., helping to register hundreds of new voters in the final days leading to the general election, operating a mobile sound car campaign and helping to coordinate advance/early voting operations that saw thousands of voters come out to vote, sometimes waiting for hours to do so because of the deliberate shenanigans of the local republican officials in charge of election operations. But true to the message, none of these antics or tactics would derail this historic movement and on November 4, 2008, the USA elected its first African American president. As Amiri Baraka wrote, "We are already in the future," and as an activist I would simply add that "we cannot afford nor choose to be spectators in this ongoing fight."

NAGUEYALTI WARREN

Mrs. Pettawah's Journal Entry,
January 20, 2009

This is the moment of sweet grace and redemption.
From Reconstruction to a new construction of nation-
hood, from out of many, one body under a groove.
This is the time to snatch the blinders off Justice
and let her see how justice is won by just us. See
all that's been done in the name of free democracy.
Hey now, this here is the *second* to heal —so many
didn't live to savor this day—but when I look up
in this cloud-patched sky, I see my husband, Mack,
King and Norma Jean, Malcolm and Rosa, Coretta
and Viola, James and Andrew, Michael and four little girls,
my grandma too and Miss Avery from down the street.
All standing at attention deep in meditation, shining,
beaming their black light, their UV rays down on US.

MARTIN ESPADA

Litany at the Tomb of Frederick Douglass
Mount Hope Cemetery, Rochester, New York
November 7, 2008

This is the longitude and latitude of the impossible;
this is the epicenter of the unthinkable;
this is the crossroads of the unimaginable:
the tomb of Frederick Douglass, three days after the election.

This is a world spinning away from the gravity of centuries,
where the grave of a fugitive slave has become an altar.
This is the tomb of a man born as chattel, who taught himself to read in secret,
scraping the letters in his name with chalk on wood; now on the anvil-flat stone
a campaign button fills the O in *Douglass*. The button says: *Obama.*
This is the tomb of a man in chains, who left his fingerprints
on the slavebreaker's throat so the whip would never carve his back again;
now a labor union T-shirt drapes itself across the stone, offered up
by a nurse, a janitor, a bus driver. A sticker on the sleeve says: *I Voted Today.*
This is the tomb of a man who rolled his call to arms off the press,
peering through spectacles at the abolitionist headline; now a newspaper
spreads above his dates of birth and death. The headline says: *Obama Wins.*

This is the stillness at the heart of the storm that began in the body
of the first slave, dragged aboard the first ship to America. Yellow leaves
descend in waves, and the newspaper flutters on the tomb, like the sails
Douglass saw in the bay, like the eyes of a slave closing to watch himself
escape with the tide. Believers in spirits would see the pages trembling
on the stone and say: look how the slave boy teaches himself to read.
I say a prayer, the first in years: that here we bury what we call
the impossible, the unthinkable, the unimaginable, now and forever. *Amen.*

Kevin Harewood

The Revolution is Being Televised!

January 20, 2009, Barack Hussein Obama was inaugurated as the 44th President of the United States. While watching the events unfold on television I wrote down flashes of memory, a collage of thoughts and images from the campaign and from my own life.

As a little boy I felt my father's exuberance when he came home from The March on Washington in 1963. At the time, I didn't know the significance of what he had experienced but knew it was something special.

I was one of the Black kids bused (or in the case of New York, "subwayed") in the late 60s and early 70s. I became a student at David A. Boody School in the predominantly Italian Bensonhurst section of Brooklyn. It was known as one of the most racist schools in New York City and we were sent into a neighborhood that was openly hostile to us. Physical attacks against Black youths were commonplace. I was identified by the school administration as someone who could help negotiate racial truces. I remember a girl in my seventh grade class declaring, "Italians are better than Blacks because we have a culture, we have spaghetti! What do Blacks have?" I wonder what she was thinking as I watched President Obama being sworn in.

James Harris of the Los Angeles Rams, Joe Gilliam of The Pittsburgh Steelers and Doug Williams of Washington Redskins were quarterbacks in the National Football League at a time when it was still believed that black men could not successfully quarterback a professional team. Williams did much to shatter that myth when he was voted MVP of the Super Bowl. Now a Black man is Quarterback of the United States of America.

On September 27, 2007, I first had the inkling that Barack Obama may have a chance at pulling off the miraculous in the 2008 Presidential election when Senator Obama brought his prodigious oratory skills to Washington Square Park in the Greenwich Village section of New York City. Washington Square Park at that time should have been a bastion of support for New York Senator Hillary Clinton and I expected a medium sized gathering comprised mostly of African Americans and young whites from nearby New York University. I was totally wrong. The park (which takes up a few city blocks) was filled to capacity with an audience that was at least 65 percent white folk from all over the demographic spectrum. Middle aged white women, the core of Senator Clinton's base, were as prevalent as African Americans and whites from the younger age groups.

Shortly after that rally, I made my final decision to not only vote for Barack Obama, but to also become a part of the magnificent grass roots volunteer effort Obama put together to make his election a reality.

Though a very proud Black American, I am not prone to vote for a candidate just because he (or she) is Black. As I've grown older, I pay more attention to the issues and less to superficialities. I vote for candidates who I feel best support the issues that are most important to me. I also study a candidate's past practice as a guideline to how they may handle themselves in the future. In the 2008 race for President, several points tipped the deck in favor of Barack Obama.

Obama appeared to be a very pensive person who gave thoughtful answers to every question posed, in contrast to the sound bite, canned, standard responses politicians often spew.

When he spoke on healthcare or education, I felt as much true sincerity for those on the lower economic and education end of the spectrum as for those with greater opportunity. Here was this Harvard Law School graudate who probably had limitless opportunities but chose to go to the South Side of Chicago as a low-paid community organizer. I saw a man who, as the son of a single mother and an absentee father, could have been a negative statistic. Instead, he used education to elevate himself to a high level of civic service. I believed he would work to secure opportunity for all youth to get a quality education. Obama seemed to know many of the same people I know. He listened to them and had deep empathy for them. He didn't patronize and was straight-forward in his conversations. He inspired optimism and accomplishment, yet would crack the whip when it needed cracking. In the words of the famous boxing referee Joe Cortez, Obama would be "firm but fair."

After I decided that Obama was indeed my man, I became engaged in the election in a manner that I had never been before. I went to our neighborhood Obama office, picked up flyers and gave them out at our block association meeting. I put a poster up in the window of my house and a bumper sticker on my girlfriend's car. I sent my twenty-five dollars to the campaign over the internet and periodically sent a few more. I spoke to my friends and sister about sending their installments of twenty-five dollars. I got my phone call list from the Obama website and made calls into places like Pennsylvania, Virginia and Ohio.

I became obsessed with watching the cable news networks, but unlike many Obama supporters, I mostly watched Fox News network. I wanted to consistently analyze what was being projected to the members of the public who were not in the same position of support for Obama that I was. From October 2007 until Election Day, November 4, 2008, I spent many hours screaming my objections when I either didn't agree with the commentary or felt it was unfair. I cheered and applauded when something was projected that showed Obama being triumphant (the fist bump, the Race Speech in Philadelphia).

On the morning of November 4th my daughter, Aura, my sister Sandra and I made sure we were at the polls to cast our votes for Obama at 5:45AM. Our polling place was the gymnasium of Public School 44, located in the Bedford Stuyvesant section of Brooklyn, New York. This is the elementary school I attended from kindergarten through fifth grade and this is where I learned what government was and also about Booker T. Washington, George Washington Carver, Harriet Tubman, Fredrick Douglass, Sojourner Truth and other Black women and men who made major contributions to our country.

On election night at around 11PM EST, I cried tears of joy as television networks projected that Barack Hussein Obama had been elected the 44th President of the United States of America.

Since the election, I continue to watch media coverage of President Obama with great interest. As important, I continue to watch our people in my travels around my Brooklyn neighborhood, my city of New York and our country. Whether I am in Brooklyn, Washington, D.C., Springfield, or Los Angeles, it is apparent to me that Obama's most valuable need for a successful Presidency is for the Black community to step up its effort toward greatness. Obama's election alone is not going to cure all our ills. Much is required from all of us. I thought about the 1970 poem by Gil Scott Heron entitled "The Revolution Will Not Be Televised." With the election of President Obama there is one thing that is clear: the most prevalent image of a Black man on television will not be that of a man in a hoodie with his hands handcuffed behind him. It will not be of a man dancing after catching a football for a touchdown, or a man rapping and smiling with a gold grill in his mouth. The most prevalent image of a Black man on television for at least the next four years will be that of a confident, strong, intelligent, cool and collected man who, at the precipice of world power, is entrusted with bettering the lives of all Americans. That is truly revolutionary!

The Secret of His Success

barack obama is the holder
of the keys to the white house
the one in washington on pennsylvania avenue
that represents the nation that his people built.
be they un-credited, relegated to back doors,
kitchens, wine cellars and after dark clean-up duty
performed in physical and mental chains carefully chanting
"yes sir, boss" with a grin and heads bowed, yet unbeaten.

today, there is a Black man with
keys to the front door of the white house.
living there with a Black woman who
stopped his young, searching heart,
helped to unlock his history, heritage and religion
gave him two daughters, a brother and
a live-in mother all darker than he is.

barack obama
birthed by a free euro-american from kansas
and a liberated african from kenya
is teaching his daughters the first lessons
that earned him the keys to the white house:
he stretched and amplified his persistent mind, traveled,
found his calling, voice and his people,
designed a path, purpose and excelled in claiming other cultures
and never, I say never,
learned the acts of niggerization
or accepted victimhood.

SHAWN L. WILLIAMS

Audacious Hope, Auspicious Signs: Barack Obama and the Third Reconstruction

Here's an understatement: witnessing the election of the first African American president was tremendously exhilarating, especially for African Americans, who just fifty years ago could not cast a vote in many places in the United States. Admittedly, even as I type the words "President Obama," I find it hard not to smile. I am also tickled by how eager black folks are to watch a presidential press conference when they never were interested before. It reminds me of when I was young and would occasionally hear elders get excited when they saw an African American, any African American, who was not making a fool of himself on television ("Come look, they got a colored on *Price is Right*").

If one would list the most celebrated events in the history of black folks in America, the election of Barack Obama would be listed between emancipation and Jack Johnson's beating Jim Jeffries. The two other events are different from one another in that while the Johnson's victory carried symbolic import, it did not influence the social condition of African Americans as freedom from legal slavery had. What makes Obama's election such a moving phenomenon was the movement that brought it about. In many ways, the Obama presidential campaign was a replication of the spirit of the African American liberation movement during the sixties. African Americans voted in record numbers, thanks to the progressive African Americans and European Americans who registered new voters and artists and entertainers who contributed their voices and their craft to what many referred to as the Obama Movement (Who was not moved by the all-star video and song "Yes, We Can" produced by will.i.am?).

Celebration is understood and was inevitable. However, as the president himself often reminds us, the difficulty of the moment should not be ignored. Yes, with the election of Barack Obama history is made, but one must recognize that the making of history is a continuously unfolding project. Only by recognizing history as ever a work-in-progress can we learn the distinction between finished lines and starting blocks. Such an understanding will help us to answer the question that must be asked following any moment of victory or a moment of defeat, which is "Where do we go from here?"

Despite what one might see emblazoned on sweatshirts, we have not yet fulfilled "the Dream" or reached "the Promised Land" that Martin Luther King, Jr. metaphorically envisioned. However, as evoked by the Obama campaign slogan we are bearing witness to change. Hopefully, Obama's election does not embody the totality of the change we can expect as what the president said during his victory speech is correct: his election alone "is not the change we seek—it is only the chance for us to make that change."

The change that we have witnessed so far is the beginning of a new historical era. The election of Barack Obama was more than just an historic event, it marked a historical shift. Not since emancipation, or the inspiration of the civil rights movement's accomplishments and the consciousness-raising of the Black Power movement, have African Americans experienced a momentous phase shift. Such transitions may at times deserve celebration but, more importantly, require circumspection. Thus, we necessarily must view the current happenings in their historical context.

America's history has revealed that its periods of progress and promise, insofar as race relations go, have been significantly shorter than its darker periods. These periods demarcate the ebb and flow of African American social and political progress. While the term "reconstruction" was originally assigned to the period during which the literal rebuilding of the union was taking place, it had been used to denote the climactic phase of the African American struggle for liberation. If we follow the idea that reconstruction involves rebuilding and indicates the periods during the history of Africans in America when America would move visibly towards the manifestation of its highest ideals and towards being truly the land of the free, then we are indeed in the wake of the Third Reconstruction.

Through the lens of African American historical scholarship, historical periods are defined based on the condition of African American social and political progression. Beginning in 1619, the slavery period[1] in the United States lasted 246 years, followed by eleven years of Reconstruction, which were swallowed up by seventy-seven years of Jim Crow. The 1954 *Brown v. Topeka, KS Board of Education* Supreme Court decision serves as the legal benchmark of what came to be known as the Second Reconstruction, which ended with the 1978 *Bakke v. University of California*, setting the climate for the legal reversal of many corrective measures (i.e. affirmative action programs) instituted in the previous era. So began what many Africana Studies scholars recognize as the second Jim Crow period. In the three hundred and sixty years since slavery was instituted, the shortest Jim Crow period lasted longer than the longest Reconstruction period.

Promise and hope, while often powerful motivators of change, can often obscure clear vision and analysis and become conducive to inaction. The challenge put before us in this Third Reconstruction is the same as that with which our forebears were faced during each of the first two Reconstructions—to transcend deeply entrenched ideological and institutional opposition and move beyond symbolic accomplishments to tangible fulfillment.

Our understanding of the first two periods of Reconstruction is necessary to enable a more successful Third Reconstruction. To keep this Reconstruction from degenerating into a regressive direction, as did the other two, would require governmental leadership fulfilling its responsibility and the masses in the grassroots staying committed to their responsibility (part of which is to keep governmental leadership responsible). The capacity of the people to maintain the momentum of progressive reform is paramount. The Second Reconstruction taught us this, as the transformation of public policy during that era was a direct result of the people's activism.

In addition to a dilapidated economy, a failed war, and diminished international respectability, President Obama has inherited the hopes of generations of African Americans and, in the minds of many of them, an obligation to the legacy of those activists and workers who blazed the trail before him. The vote for "change," as indicated in the results of the election, is a call for rebuilding. Despite the prevalence of optimism, there is abounding concern, if not fear that Barack Obama may become the object of change rather than the agent of change. Indeed, the entering president's choices of less progressive cabinet appointees lead Cornel West to wonder publically whether President Obama is "reluctant to step into the age of

Obama." The question before us then is whether the president will be able to move America toward the kind of egalitarianism envisioned and pursued collectively by African Americans since the time of American enslavement. In a word, will Barack Obama fulfill the hopes and aspirations invested in him?

Based on much of his rhetoric, Barack Obama sees himself as a Reconstruction president. President Obama has liberally infused his rhetoric with invocations from America's previous Reconstruction eras. Indeed, he has invoked the rhetorical posture of the dominant figures of each of the two previous Reconstruction periods: Abraham Lincoln and Martin King.

Since the beginning of his candidacy, Obama has overtly identified with Lincoln, who was faced with the task of preserving and reconstructing the union. Like the president who sought to lead the First Reconstruction, President Obama made overt moves to heal rifts preceding his election. President Obama named the chief rival for his party's presidential nomination, Hillary Clinton, as Secretary of State; Lincoln had done the exact same, naming Williams Seward to that position (which, given Seward's contempt for his president's authority, turned out to be one of Lincoln's worst decisions). Most notably, during the first Reconstruction, Lincoln included representatives of the defunct Confederacy in his administration.

Superficial commonalities with Lincoln, whether intended or coincidental, will have no significant bearing on President Obama's ability to effectively reconstruct America—which, incidentally, is more than putting the nation back together (its most obvious meaning in Lincoln's time), but rebuilding the nation into something better (the intention of African American liberation activists and their allies). While there are practical lessons that he can learn from his predecessors, the new president's best lessons and inspirations can be found not in the legacy of past presidents, but in the legacy of African American liberation workers and leaders who were sincerely invested in the struggle to create a society that was just in visible deed rather than vocalized creed. Barack Obama won the hearts of African Americans not because he is African American, but because he is perceived as being *of* African Americans. (Condoleesa Rice or Shelby Steele could not have gained nearly as much African American support.) Conversely, some of the apprehension felt by some whites was based on his identification with the African American community, especially some of the more "unapologetically black" elements.

The best value of the African American experience is that it offers a worldview rooted in the sensibilities of the downtrodden and a tradition of creating a more just and equitable society. Wisely, and with apparent sincerity, Obama has never diminished his connection to African America. There have, however, been efforts by others to minimize, if not deny, that connection. In cyberspace and mainstream media, some raised questions concerning Obama's identity as an African American because his mother was white. As is the case with much of the assessment of Obama and other African Americans, such questions are raised out of ignorance of history. Many African Americans of renown were born to a white parent. Frederick Douglass, whose father was a white slave master, has never had his identity as an African American questioned. Strangely, another way membership in the African American community has been questioned is because of his Kenyan father, whose birth on the African continent renders his son not "one of those" (i.e., a descendant of the Africans who were enslaved in America for nearly three hundred years).

As President Obama rightly indicates, meeting the core needs of the American public means meeting the needs of African Americans. Look among those in need of health care access and in financial crisis and one finds more than a few black folks. When it comes to environmental issues, the effects of climate change threaten all human life. (For evidence of the impact of failing to address natural threats, see Katrina.) African Americans are always numbered (and disproportionately so) among those suffering in America; such has always been the case. Just as it has always been so that liberation movements of African Americans served to benefit all other Americans. For example, the efforts to create schools for southern African Americans that began during the First Reconstruction led to the establishment of public education systems in the South. Activism during the Second Reconstruction brought into being legislation that provides legal protection for all U.S. citizens against any form of discrimination.

The hope that President Obama has inspired is not entirely of his making, and any lasting fulfillment of that hope will not be either. Certainly, public policy influenced by the judicial opposition to affirmative action and hostile or indifferent presidential leadership, most notably during the Reagan administration, ended the second Reconstruction and began the second Jim Crow period. But what may have also contributed to that transition was the failure of African Americans to transform hope and fire into sustainable institutions.

Regarding racial matters, there is an obvious expectation of a greater sensitivity from the new president. He was indeed sensitive enough to walk the line between black folks' concerns and white folks' fears. During the election campaign, he managed to skillfully circumvent the issue of racism in America without denying its potency. Barack Obama is right in his call that Americans should see beyond their differences to address common concerns and challenges. However, some of his comments during the most trying controversies affecting his campaign suggest that seeing beyond differences should mean ignoring differences, and that looking forward necessitates turning a blind eye toward the past. To downplay the issue of racism observed by some of his supporters, Obama has criticized these same supporters saying that they focus on what's wrong with America more so than what's right with America." To boast about what's "right about this country" and ignore "what's wrong about this country" is to embrace utopian idealism at the expense of critical truth. Of course, part of the president's job description is reflecting American pride; thus, his job does not offer the freedom, that we civilians have to "keep it real."

I would venture to say that many African Americans were very conscious of the predicament that candidate Obama was in. Many of us assumed that he did not have the freedom to be as forthright on discussions of race as we might have liked. He could not, for instance, say to what degree he might agree with Jeremiah Wright's condemnation of the moral arrogance of the United States. I believe it was an understanding of this predicament that was the reason African Americans forgave candidate Obama for what could be taken as slights or even insults. While I did not agree with those who took issue with Obama's Father's Day speech in which he mentioned that too many African American men shirk their family responsibilities, we did let him slide when he said Jeremiah Wright's remarks, including his expressed admiration of Louis Farrakhan, "rightly offended all Americans." The (assumedly unintentional) implication then is that those who were in agreement with Wright, and that includes a good number of African Americans, are somehow not Americans.

Now that the election is over, hopefully, African Americans will exercise the freedom to offer critique of our president that is not always congratulatory. There are some concerns regarding President Obama that are troubling—his to-date uncritical support of the State of Israel and his subtle yielding to the current political climate to engage in macho posturing when addressing issues of international terrorism. And I am still listening out for him to substantively address critical issues relative to Africa, specifically debt forgiveness.

The obligation heaped upon Barack Obama calls to mind the advice that Malcolm X offered to Muhammad Ali (while he was Cassius Clay) when he emerged as a symbol of hope for the African world community after winning the world championship. Malcolm wrote to the new champion and emerging folk hero, "Because a billion of our people in Africa, Arabia, and Asia love you blindly, you must now be forever aware of your tremendous responsibilities to them." Not since Muhammad Ali has an African American, or any American, inspired the hopes and embodied the aspirations of people throughout the world as Obama has.

The African American people's faith in Barack Obama should be tempered by critical vigilance. As a self-recognized beneficiary of the African American liberation struggle, his debt to that struggle can only be paid by continuing its legacy to building a just society, safe environment, and elevating humanity to higher levels. The hope for full liberation of African American people cannot rest solely on the Obama administration. That hope rests with the people who put him in office. The fight for liberation began before this presidency, and it shall continue on afterward. In the meantime, the president should be expected, supported, and as necessary pressured to be the agent of change he professed to be during his election campaign.

Note

1. The period known as the Holocaust of Enslavement is actually the third period of African American history. The first two are the African Exploration Period, beginning about 500 BC, and the African/European Exploration Period, beginning in 1492.

SHARAN STRANGE

Inaugural

How to chronicle the swoon, the gut-strung
      expectation of that day? How to capture
          the sagacity of a swagger announcing change
             like the tremolo of a new Blues… How to croon

…the rhythm's shift—slight, though enough
        —that we might dare to breathe, loosen, lean toward
          one another, cultivate a human wealth?

Though America will gobble him down like any savior—liminal,
                                    magical,
                     sacrificial
              one whose richness,
         like chocolate eaten at bedtime,
makes the stomach queasy after initial greedy relish—

          we dare to imagine the mitosis of more
       than a million glossy headshots assuaging
a collective ache.

What promise I gleaned from my place among the groundswell:

Real acts in the marketplace of simulacra that politics has become—

        Love in his gaze, amidst millions, in the void of a chilled day,
           and his wink to Love beyond the frame…
Love in her gloved hand, crossing the boundary of ceremony and pomp,
           defying a million editing shots,
              the sure heft
                 caressing his shoulder….

My breath quickened by that historic exchange, *that* wealth.

ANTOINETTE BRIM

We Winter Still

For those standing on the Mall to witness the inauguration of
President Barack Obama

We winter   holding fast to dreams
while robins perch   in budding trees
and shadows smooth the skyscape.

We winter until
our breath   becomes brittle
and the children ask: *why are we*
standing in the cold   still?

A chorus of mothers
half mumble/half hum:
Ooh child, things are gonna get easier.

We do what we know:
        Wait!   until we just can't stand much more.
We do what we do:
        Wait longer!   for a healing
under an unclouded sky. Our someday.

All about us is noise,
but the ancestors swell silent.

Today was summoned by blood and water.
We have turned the corner and run into
ourselves swaying to the chorus
of mothers who half mumble/half hum:
Ooh child, things are gonna get easier.

I see the robins
perched in budding treetops.
But people know. Our people know.
It's still winter. So, we winter still.
We gather our coats into one clenched fist
to draw them up underneath our chins.
In the other hand, we hold a promissory note,
a noble piece of paper, emblazoned
with one word: *hope.*

It is winter still, but I see robins
perched in the budding treetops.
It is winter still, but we are standing
so close, I feel warmth.

Consider the changing sky. Today is the prayer,
every prayer ever sung in a field, juke joint, church or jail.
Schoolhouse, roadhouse. Every wail of every whip now
joins the chorus of mothers and the swell of our ancestors to sing:

Ooh child, things are gonna get easier.

MALAIKA ADERO

The Reckoning: A Prayer by the People

"The day of reckoning is here," said Barack Obama in his address to the joint session of Congress and a television viewership. This was the day after the 141st birthday of W.E.B DuBois and three days after the 44th anniversary of the assassination of Malcolm X—two men who cut paths that became the super highway that this Black American man took to become the 44th President of the United States. Elegba has opened the gate.

My household sat and watched the live broadcast fully attentive and filled with pride. Heretofore, if we had watched a presidential address at all, we would have spent a good bit of the time talking back to the idiot box as if in a neighborhood movie theatre, mocking the characters who stand and scream in submission to the villains. Our leader, in this moment, was standing firm, speaking truth as the power. Sango.

We chuckled even at the giddiness of the president's opposition. Republicans and Democrats alike were jumping to their feet to applaud, seeming to take his verbal smack-downs to greed as willingly as they swallowed his talk of "big ideas" and the notion that we, America, have "the ability to shape our world for good," not for ill.

White people love themselves a rock star and Barack Obama is It, for now. But everybody knows the star child gets love in increments of 15 minutes—not even the 30 days that star presidents are said to be allowed. Obama's movements reveal that he knows this too, he is—with every press conference, measure and swipe of his pen—striking chords of resonance, while his music is hot.

Black folk, well, we love anyone who can use language, swagger, spiritual—and every other kind of—intelligence, courage, cool and fearlessness. Ourselves at our best. This is the key to Obama's success: we saw our Martin, Malcolm, Stokely, Angela—ourselves in him, Michelle and their children. We saw Iowans seduced. We reckoned for the better part of two years, watching a caravan of states grow and nay-sayers shrink. We elected ourselves a Black First Family in the First World. Grandmother Obama hands him the oxtail fly whisk. Grandmother Robinson brings the children. The siblings are the chorus of English, Indonesian, French, Cantonese, German, Hebrew, Swahili, Luo, Gullah, Igbo. Michelle Robinson is Isis, holding the sky above our Sun King. Is Osun in lemon grass. Is beholding to Obatala in white. We recite the 99 names of Allah, Jesus, Oludumare and give thanks in every language on the planet. And, we are most patient, when we can see down the road—a resting place.

Look at how long the heretofore was. Since the 19th century we've been running for office and sometimes winning. The post-slavery, Reconstruction era U.S. Congress had some Black folk representing. Then came the backhoe of Jim Crow and Black Codes and the supersizing of white supremacy to dig up the road. In the 1960s we mixed the asphalt of the Civil Rights Movement and laid Black struggle from the Edmund Pettus Bridge to the Mall in the Capitol. In the 1970s we took revolution to the bridge from Oakland to Harlem. We did that when we reckoned and when we were tireless. Ogun.

Reckon: means to count or compute, to consider as being, to figure, to take into account, to consider as being, rely with confident expectancy. Black people in the early to mid 20th century considered expanding their presence beyond the South to claim recognition as Americans and took to the roads creating the Great Migrations. It was not legislation that freed our minds when we were fearlessness. We gripped the fly whisk.

Black people like my grandparents considered the land they had already worked and reckoned they would remain in the South confident with expectancy that they would achieve the vote and the ballot would one day count in their favor. Texana and Grundy, Ben and Caroline, Alvin and Eula Crump; John and Allie Caldwell Green; Mack Collins, True Ralph and Ollie Blue and others of my ancestors are the ones who hovered around my head whispering "this can happen." My Uncle Joe Louis Franklin Crump, who didn't make it to age 50, but took me along with him to a political protest at age 10, spoke to me from the other side echoing the others: You can continue the reckoning, laying the pavement of free expression and self-determination from interstate to international.

I began counting the ways that we drive our way into the Oval Office when I heard Obama speak at the Democratic Convention in 2004, channeling Malcolm and Martin in his look and sound. When I read his *Dreams of My Father* I gathered how he got his name and claim to Africa.

My own late father has risen out of his cosmic seat, no longer believing us to be excluded from the Chosen People. This is our Day of Recognition.

My brother Robert held a flag for the first time—with pride—on election night. But there is nothing post-racial about this new day. We have rather shifted from the shoulder to the fast lane of America, relegating toll booths like poll taxes to history and opening up the gates to let the questions of race be addressed like all other crisis of now. There is nothing to fear but color-blindness and cowardice. Let's speak up—in the tradition of a nation born from revolution and a people characterized by emancipation.

Election Day in Harlem, I met my neighbors anew. We stood together patiently, waiting to caste our lot with our self interests. We gathered into parties, in our institutions, in the streets in our living rooms. We embraced each other—across the color line, for the first time—in a new way. Four years ago, I read a bumper sticker that said: Bush/Cheney, I vote the Bible. Now, the Right Wing is broken. The Book is wide open and a multitude on the same page. In the headlines, we call King the Dreamer, Obama, the Dream. The Day of Reckoning.

Inauguration Day in the District, we watched the revolution being televised. The Family assembled: Grandmother Obama brought the oxtail fly whisk. The artists, photographers, vendors and publishers are inspired by the voice of the Speaker in Chief and the dance of the multitude in the streets. Beautiful, but merely ceremony. Our grandparents would say, I reckon we must get to work. Seize the new. I now wear a watch with the president's face: Nation time.

Looking for the Right to Be. Checking for the Left to organize. Race people rise. Don't just criticize. Arrest poverty, arrest greed, arrest racism, arrest war, arrest slavery. Advance planet Earth and her humanity. Fly your whisk. Wave your flags. This is our time, the leader is Barack Hussein Obama, the leader is you, me, the leaders of the New Free World Order Speak. Jerejef, Modupe, Danke, Merci, Gracia, Asante Sana, Thank you Jesus, Allah u Akbar, Amen.

LITA HOOPER

The Poem My Son Will Write One Day

My hand pressed into my mother's as I stood
beside her, barely reaching the tip of her shoulder.

We two-stepped forward, careful not to touch
the backs of shoes ahead: brown loafers, white sneakers.

It was cold that day, barely a blue patch visible in the pearly sky.
Still we waited in line, determined, this important day.

Sister and daddy behind us, a woman on a cell phone close enough.
My old friend, Impatience, tugged, then gave way to a voice

wafting along the orderly mass. "Never thought I'd see the day!"
My heart dictated a strange code, a bird fluttered nearby.

The immediacy of it all—the moment swelling like the bird's wings
as it ascended, leaving us in communal expectation.

Head thrown back, I watched as smoky gray puffs
devoured the dark, soaring thing.

DEMETRICE ANNTÍA WORLEY

On This Day, at This Moment—A Ghazal

In Africa…the concept of time was elastic and
encompassed events that had already taken place, as
well as those that would occur immediately.

—John Mbiti

Election Day 2008: I have waited one hour and forty-eight minutes outside,
in America.
A Black woman wanting change, driver's license and voter's registration
card in hand. My vote in America.

A blank-eyed African leans back against ship's coarse wood rail, slides over.
His walnut body beds on white bones, joins
19 million Africans building Middle Passage Bridge. A slavery traffic
footnote in America.

January 2009, *U.S. Supreme Court Will Hear Challenge to 1964 Voting*
Rights Act. Prayers—
to God, Yahweh, Allah, Nzambi, Bonkongo goddess of justice— for a sound
lifeboat in America.

Slave cabin's darkness blankets his bloody back. Fire burns as his whipped
body glistens, a fever's sweat. Wife's thin hands
dip cloth, bathe wounds, spread balm. Holds child. Leans low, whispers,
stay alive—she knows slavery's antidote in America.

U. S. House of Representatives gives its regrets to Black Americans, July
2008, for *wrongs*
committed against them and their ancestors who suffered under slavery
and Jim Crow. More rote in America.

Robert Kennedy forecasts a U.S. *Negro* President in forty years, *we are making progress. We will*
not accept the status quo; In 1968, seismic rumble, a thought terremote, in America.

[*T*]*his nation . . . shall have a new birth of freedom,* Abraham Lincoln divines, June 1865. *[G]overnment*
of the people, for the people, by the people, shall not perish. Faith stronger than banknotes in America.

Birmingham, May 1964: Black and White people sit on warm street, sing, *We shall overcome.* On evening
news—dogs gnaw arms, legs; water hoses bounce bodies across tar—world sees racism's scapegoat in America.

Barack Obama's inaugural voice splits winter air, *[T]oday, we must...begin again the work of remaking America.*
Optimism's boldness catches in Black, Hispanic, Native, Asian, White collective throat, in America.

E. ETHELBERT MILLER

The Day the Earth Stood Still

Some of us took Octavia Butler
and Samuel Delany books off the shelf.

Churches closed their doors as if men
were saying their prayers for the last time.

In was a cold day in January. Cold enough
for history to stay indoors under a quilt.

Many of us. Maybe millions went down
to the Mall to hear Obama.

I stood behind Duke Ellington and Billy
Strayhorn. Duke was composing on the spot.

Sacred music was in the air. I wanted
to lift every voice and sing.

I wanted to hear the thunder and watch
the first drops of a new American rain.

GLORIA HOUSE

Annual Martin Luther King Day
Observation and March

Central Methodist Church Detroit

January 19, 2009

I would like to begin by expressing my thanks to the MLK Day planning committee for inviting me to speak. It has been forty years since Dr. King's martyrdom, and for some of us gathered here, forty years of community organizing, activist work and sacrifice, before arriving now at this dream of 2008, Barack Obama's election to the Presidency. We cannot speak of a direct line of connection between our civil rights and liberation movements and Obama's victory. Our activist objectives never proposed the election of a President. We didn't contemplate or even fantasize about such a possibility.

We were too disillusioned with the U.S. government to think that the Presidency could ever actually serve the needs of people. And we were too busy! Too busy organizing to protect our communities and ensure their survival, too busy mobilizing to stop police brutality, very busy trying to hold on to our city resources as they were being ripped off by suburban scams, too busy trying to protect and educate our children in a school system that was being dismantled by the State so suburban contractors and others could deplete the budget surplus, and so we would finally lose control of the school system all together.

We were too busy demanding equal access for people of color to jobs and higher education, too busy trying to hold on to jobs in spite of the hostility we faced in the offices and factories where we worked, very busy sustaining our families and relationships as we took to the streets to express our outrage and resistance to the inhumane policies of the U.S. government; busy organizing opposition to the war on Iraq when the majority of Americans were mesmerized by Bush's cowboy aggression and stupendous lies about weapons of mass destruction, and most recently, we have been too busy organizing to stop home foreclosures as Wall Street collapsed.

We were working so hard, many of us lost health, lost our families, lost our minds. We were so determined to speak out against human rights violations when others were silent that many of us found ourselves locked away in America's dungeons without hope of release; some of us were murdered outright by the State.

Occupied by these many pressing realities in our communities, in the forty years of struggle since Martin, we didn't dream of an African American President; but then that is the miracle of *revolutionary* change!

C.L.R. James, the beloved Trinidadian historian and revolutionary thinker, once mentioned to a group of us young movement workers that the qualitative social changes we have worked for as activists may come suddenly, and sometimes unexpectedly, following the laws of dialectics, that after a long period of struggle with certain issues and problems, there's the possibility that we will witness something quite new come into being, a change that takes us much farther in human organization and spiritual development than we could have foreseen.

I like to think about this qualitative leap of change in the way Dudley Randall, Detroit's first poet laureate, wrote about it. He envisioned this new social reality as opening like a beautiful red flower of revolution ("Roses and Revolution").

The work we undertook—to reveal to our community the life destructive contradictions inherent in capitalism and the popular attachment to the mythology of the American dream, to demand the release of political prisoners, to pull our sons out of the jaws of the military forces that we call our local police, the work in solidarity with the liberation movements in the Third World; the work to cultivate gardens to feed our communities, the discipline to study our history, the imagination to create rituals that would nurture and sustain our spirituality; the effort to learn how to integrate our spirits and our political strivings, how to pace ourselves to be able to walk the long road to freedom. All this work has borne fruit, not as much as we wished perhaps, and not always in the specific ways that we intended, but nevertheless, it has engendered a different consciousness that has touched many Americans outside our immediate organizing circles, like the blooming of that immense red flower, consciousness of alternative ways to live as human beings, and this consciousness, an extension of Dr. King's legacy and the spirit of the 60s freedom fighters, provided the ethos in which a Barack Obama could grow up, offered him an alternative set of values to American corporate elitism, inspired him to work as a community organizer, and radicalized his consciousness to the extent that he could envision new forms of leadership, could envision even the Presidency of the United States, in a fundamentally altered way. So, indeed, Dr. King's spirit hovers over the inauguration of this President, along with the spirits of those warriors before Martin and since.

How can we characterize this qualitative shift in the American political ethos? And how will it influence our future work as activists and cultural workers? First of all, let's say that U.S. imperialism has ripped its pants irreparably and all its ugliness is shonuff on front street. Can I get an amen? Even the most rabid supporters of U.S. imperialism, cultural supremacy and white chauvinism have been driven into silence as they watched the astonishing deceit of U.S. foreign and domestic policy exposed on their television screens: the outright lies concerning weapons of mass destruction in Iraq, the manipulation of intelligence, the plundering of Iraq for cultural treasures and oil, the greed of cabinet officials, the dumbing down of responses to the most complicated issues of human and planetary survival such as global warming, unjust detention and torture—and the rationalization of torture as essential to national security–all these human rights travesties are now an open book for the American public. So we activists don't have to work so hard disclosing them and coaxing our neighbors to see *the real*. We can take off from another starting point.

The perpetrators have been exposed, the President and his cabinet– most recently by defectors from their own ranks, and their criminality is in full view. When they are called out, they answer simply, "So what?" So what? Dick Chaney replied disdainfully when reminded that the majority of American people now oppose the war in Iraq. And "so what" appeared to be the response of the administration to the unprecedented suffering of Katrina victims. So what? Such a mundane response, expressing such startling indifference to human life, human suffering, human rights. These criminals no longer bother with masks, revealing a blatant callousness which makes it impossible for American citizens to go on denying the destructive, belligerent nature of U.S. policy and practices in the world. The cavalier indifference of the Bush administration to Constitutional law and correct international conduct have forced naïve Americans finally to let go of the myth of the U.S. as international savior, good cop, good Samaritan to the underdeveloped world, as the truth has become easily accessible through communication technology. We used to have to do extensive research for our teach-ins—consulting the foreign press, scouring radical journals. Now, the details of domestic and foreign political abuses are in our faces in the local newspapers!

We are *living* the effects of the imperialist policies and globalization in our joblessness, our hunger, our lost homes, our chronic, unattended illnesses, our early deaths, and we can draw a straight line from our own conditions to the decisions of those leaders who no longer even try to hide their indifference.

The Bush cabinet has betrayed the American people, and are abandoning the nation in a state of total chaos, with cutbacks and collapses in all sectors of the national life: the greatest economic crisis since the Depression, brought on in large part by fraud; 90 percent of the nation's wealth deposited in the pockets of only 10 percent of the population; massive unemployment, two ongoing wars, with the lives of over 4,000 soldiers squandered *in the unjust war on Iraq*, unknown thousands of civilians killed, and in the last three weeks, a monstrously irresponsible position of hands-off neutrality in response to the Israeli offensive on the Palestinians.

It is possible that Barack Obama will walk into the most beleaguered White House ever in the history of this country. Nevertheless, he will manage because he has mastered the necessary leadership skills, he has worked daily in communities to help ordinary citizens empower themselves, and this work has shaped the way he approaches government. If we believe there is such a thing as personal destiny, Obama serves as a brilliant illustration. With a name that means *blessing,* he has assumed the world's stage with corresponding attributes, attitudes and dispositions in direct opposition to those of the outgoing U.S. President.

Barack Obama values thought, he thinks deeply, he *actually believes* the Constitution is the law of the land! He values imagination, he values knowledge of history; he values ritual and ceremony as essential unifying activities, *he appears to value truth*; he knows what it means to be marginal, to be poor, to be powerless. He knows how it feels to be despised—for reasons of race, or for simply being different.

No former U.S. President has brought such a remarkable set of gifts: awareness of the struggles of hard-working people, extraordinary intelligence and insight, attention to the lessons of history, and the *broadest possible appreciation of the cultures and rights of people worldwide.* All that said, no wonder we are experiencing what Vernon Jordan called "a national irrational exuberance." Of course, we are happy! But I would suggest that we remain realistic as we celebrate this historic moment.

Let's be level-headed about what Obama will be able to do within the restraining parameters of the Presidency. Though he is the first African American President, let's be clear: he won't *belong* to us African Americans. He can't. Make us proud, yes, let us smile to see the President walking into the White House with that cool Black man swagger that is so fine? Yes, we can revel in that, as we revel in Michelle's African woman's kind of gorgeousness, but they cannot make us their favorites, so to speak, defending us and speaking out on our behalf at each injustice we may suffer. Michelle and Barack belong to the *whole country*, and would fail their calling if they didn't make that clear. That said, what is so special, then, about having Obama as President?

What is important is that now we have a conscious African American man in the White House with whom we can work as change agents, as revolutionaries, in complimentarity rather than in opposition. We can organize and mobilize to ensure the passage of ideas the President has proposed for the betterment of conditions of health, education, and employment, not only for people of color, but for the entire nation. In other words, hopefully we have a leader whom we can support from the ground up. He will need our support because, no matter his personal convictions or intentions, his proposals must make their way through the contentiousnes of Congress, and we can assume that once the inaugural honeymoon is over, he will face very antagonistic forces. We must be ready to bring pressure from the ground up for those measures we recognize as beneficial.

Though we have a President with a new kind of social consciousness, we have to go on carrying out our work on the ground. The President cannot take to the streets in protest when human rights have been trampled. We can! Perhaps the President, for reasons of international diplomacy, cannot say the bombing of Gaza by the Israelis is of such disproportion as to constitute massacre or genocide. *We can say that! And we must!*

Let's hold Obama to the work he can do within the limitations of his office, and let's continue to pursue in our own practice some of the most important objectives we have formulated over years of struggle (that he has had the good sense to borrow):

Boldly project new visions, new forms of social organization and communication networks;

Refuse to be intimidated by the old conventions, old expectations, by others' attempts to ridicule our trials and errors;

Challenge ourselves to discover innovative solutions to old problems, to enact surprising, imaginative strategies;

Trust in our capacity to create a more human society, where people cooperate, work, and envision more fulfilling, loving ways of interacting across racial, ethnic and religious barriers;

Reject the dumbing down of our minds, of our national culture, the degradation and desecration of our bodies and sexuality that characterize contemporary popular culture in the U.S.;

Teach our children self-respect, self-esteem and respect for others; insist that they learn basic civility and a preference for peace-making;

Reaffirm the essential roles of intelligence, creative thought, and imagination in the advancement of human life and encourage everyone–especially our children–to develop and contribute their artistic abilities;

Strive for honesty and transparency in all our work and interactions;

Continue to stand and mobilize for peace and justice among nations, particularly across boundaries of race, religion and ideology.

In many of his campaign speeches, Obama inspired the crowds by saying, "We are the change we've been waiting for." *I* say, *we*, those of us here today, *have not been waiting*. We have been *working*, and this period of "national, irrational exuberance" is a good time to celebrate the fruits of our labor. Oprah and Toni Morrison, the Nobel Prize-winning writer, have said that Barack is the One. Perhaps, but he is *only* one. We are many. And the momentum to create a new world requires the unity of many. Let's honor Dr. King's legacy and the spirits of all our freedom fighters throughout our history by insisting on holding up the freedom banner in all the decisive moments, challenges, and struggles of our lives.

Long live the spirit of the Rev. Dr. Martin Luther King, Jr. and long live our commitment to justice and freedom.

Thank you!

Kwame Dawes

New Day

1

Obama, January 1, 2009

Already the halo of grey covers his close-cropped head.
Before, we could see the pale glow of his skull, the way
he kept it close, now the grey—he spends little time in bed,
mostly he places things in boxes or color coded trays,
and calculates the price of expectation—the things promised
all eyes now on him: the winning politician's burden.
On the day he makes his speech he will miss
the barber shop, the quick smoke in the alley, the poem
found in the remainder box, a chance to just shoot
some hoops, and those empty moments to remember
that green rice paddy where he used to sprint, a barefoot
screaming boy, all legs, going home to the pure
truth of an ordinary life, that simple place where, fatherless,
he found comfort in the wisdom of old broken soldiers.

2

How Legends Begin

This is how legends begin—the knife slitting the throat
of a hen, the blood, the callous pragmatism of eating
livestock grown for months, the myth of a father, a boat
ride into the jungle, a tongue curling then flinging
back a language alien as his skin; the rituals
of finding the middle ground, navigating a mother's
mistakes, a father's silence, a world's trivial
divisions, the meaning of color and nation—negotiator

---

of calm, a boy tutored in the art of profitable charm;
this is how legends begin and we will tell this, too,
to the children lined up with flags despite the storms
gathering, children who will believe in the hope of blue
skies stretched out behind the mountain of clouds;
and he will make language to soothe the teeming crowds.

3

Waking Up American, November 5, 2008

She says she never saw him as black, unlike his mother
who said *she* did. She says she saw him as colorless,
just a man, unlike his white mother who touched his father's
face, the deep brown earth, the glow. She says it's best
to see him as simply a human in this country that shed
long ago the pernicious sting of race, she says, and I
call her a tenderhearted, dreamer, a sweet liar, I say,
a white-lie teller who would rather tell this bland lie
before admitting that walking down King Street
the morning after the votes were counted, she was
scared, but proud, so giddy with the wild beat
of her heart, knowing that her country paused
for an instant and did something grand, made a black
man president, such a miracle, such beautiful magic.

4

Punch-line

I have asked this of them year after year, a punch-line
waiting to happen with clockwork consistency—
raise your hand if you can remember a time
you believed that even you could take the presidency;
yes, you, blacks, poor, women, Latinos—was it when
you were four, five, six? And the believers all

would raise their hands. So the second question:
how many now think you have the wherewithal
to be the chief today—and up go four hands:
a dreamer, a liar, a clown, a madman. What went wrong?
How did you all mess up? Well, it's messed up now, it's gone
now that a black man has done it! Cancel class, time to hang
a poor joke; can't complain about oppression no more;
we've got to recalibrate who is the man now, that's for sure.

5

Palmetto

Of course, my home has kept its promise to itself;
the one that made Eartha Kitt, Chubby Checker, Althea Gibson,
James Brown all pack their bags, clean out their shelves,
never to look back, not once. They found their homeless songs,
like people who have forgotten where their navel-strings
were buried. We kept the promise that made those who stayed learn
to fight with the genius of silence, the subterfuge of rings
of secret flames held close to the heart, kindling the slow burn
of resistance. But good news: despite the final state count,
we know that the upheaval of all things still brought grace
here where pine trees bleed and palmettos suck up the brunt
of blows, and so we can now hum the quiet solace
of victory with a surreptitious shuffle, a quick, quick-step
for you, Smoking Joe, Dizzy, James, and Jessie, slide, slide, now step.

6

Confession

Here is my confession, then, the one I keep inside me—
while the crowds gather in Washington, I will admit this:
it is enough that it happened, more than enough that we see

him standing there shattering all our good excuses: no, not bliss,
not some balm over the wounds that still hurt, but it is enough
to say that we saw it happen, the thing we thought wouldn't,
and we did it even if we did not want to do it. And that is tough,
yes, but it is good and grand and beautiful and new. And,
more, it is enough, no matter what comes next, that a man
who knows the blues, knows the stop-time of be-bop,
who's asked from inside out the meaning of blood and skin,
is, let's just say it, standing there, yes, standing at the top
of the world—it is enough for tomorrow; and yes he is tough
and yes he is smart, but mostly it is sweet and more than enough.

7
On Having a Cool President

He will not be the buffoon and clown; he's too cool for that.
His cool is the art of ease, the way we drain out tension;
the way we make hard seem easy, seem like it ought.
Cool is not seeing the burn in the fluid grace of execution.
Cool is knowing how to lean back and let it come,
but always ready for it to come. He will be no minstrel show
fool, but a man who shows, in the midst of chaos, unruffled calm.
Like, *what-does-he-know-that-we-don't-know?*
Like, *I-can-be-brighter-than-you-and-still-be-down*, cool.
Like some presidential cool; a cool that maybe hasn't been seen
in the White House before. You see, he is a nobody's fool,
kind of cool, the one that makes a gangsta lean look so clean,
kind of cool. That's what we have now, and to be honest,
you can call this cool what you want. Me , I call it blessed.

8
Lincoln, January 1, 1865

I think now of that other Illinois man, pacing the creaking boards
of the musty mansion, cradling a nation's future in his head,
the concussion of guns continuing, the bloody hordes
of rebels like ghouls in his dreams; he, too, avoids the bed;
tomorrow the hundred days will be over, a million
souls will be free, a million pieces of property pilfered
from citizens, a million laborers worth their weight in bullion
promised a new day across the border, a million scared
owners, a million calamities, all with the flow of ink
from his pen. This is the path of the pragmatist who would
be savior, the genius act of simple war, the act to sink
an enemy, and yet hallelujahs will break out like loud
ululations of freedom. *Uneasy lies the head...*, he knows—
this is how our leaders are born, how we find our heroes.

Malia at Lincoln's Desk

Malia's thin brown arms move
with certainty, crisp strides toward
Lincoln's bedroom until she rests
books, papers, pencils and pens

on simple black slab of wood topped
with modest shelf. She looks at delicate
whispers of prints speckling the wallpaper,
imagines the height of tall men's shadows,

admires mahogany shine under fingertips with a deep breath set on thinking
big thoughts swelling in her papers,
homework for her, history for others.

She primly folds her skirt under lean legs,
smiles like any schoolgirl should at a desk.
Her quiet moment, private as a diary with tiny
lock and key. A soft straight feather of her hair

meanders to the corner of her smile, as she picks
up a pen, writes, listens to the murmurs of cooks,
sharecroppers, firehoses, typists and speechmakers,
and the underestimated weaponry of pens still

scratching out urgings implied by Emancipation.

NATHAN MCCALL

White America's Trauma

Just before the election made Barack Obama the most powerful person on the planet, an online publication, *The Root,* ran an article topped with this headline:

"Win or Lose, How Will We Cope?"

The subtitle of the piece revealed that the writer, noted black psychiatrist Dr. Alvin Poussaint, was offering counsel to the nation's 37 million African Americans on "managing the stress of history." Although Poussaint's counsel was thoughtful and welcomed, his advice now seems like a case of the right idea, wrong crowd.

True, blacks everywhere were stressed by the suspense of the election. After all, this was an event of monumental import. Still, we as a people are veterans at managing extreme stress. Blacks have mastered the art of coping for four centuries now.

As for coping and stress, it appears white folks, much more than us, could stand some time on the couch. Since Obama's historic victory I've heard stories that bear that out–tales of how some white bosses, shaken by this upending of their universe, have been gruff and spiteful toward blacks in the workplace. While much of the nation remains giddy with glee, millions of whites out there are dazed, and traumatized.

Witness the break with sanity that gripped a *New York Post* cartoonist just three months after the final votes revealed the score. He drew a picture of a policeman who plugged bullet holes into a monkey, which lay sprawled and splattered in blood. As the ape lay dying, the cop's partner, standing nearby, commented, casually, "They'll have to find someone else to write the next stimulus bill."

Despite the paper's denials (prompted, of course, by protests led by Rev. Al Sharpton and filmmaker Spike Lee), it's clear the cartoon reflected the symbolic assassination of President Obama. The only thing more outrageous than the cartoon itself was the fact that it was printed in a mainstream newspaper. Newspapers have editors in place as checks and balances to prevent publication of such mean-spirited filth. Yet editors at the *Post* allowed its cartoonist to indulge his racist wishful thinking because, one can assume, it mirrored *their* racist wishful thinking. Besides reflecting tastelessness beyond comprehension, that cartoon is a jolting reminder of the depth of America's racial pathology.

The New York Post episode was barely a month old when more presidential monkey business reared its ugly head. In Coral Gables, Florida, a Barnes & Noble book store exhibited a disturbing window display, which made its way to the internet. A book titled *Monkeys* was placed strategically in the center of the display. The book featured a huge mug shot of a bewhiskered chimp gracing the cover. In an unmistakable reference to the age-old stereotype that has dogged blacks, *Monkeys* was surrounded by several photos and books about President Obama, his wife and children. *Monkeys.*

What these and other public tantrums suggest is that while many Americans are celebrating Obama's victory as a promising step toward racial progress, the emergence of a black president is generating a meltdown in other quarters across the land. No doubt, this thing is sending shockwaves through the tortured systems of some whites, many of whom believe black progress comes at their expense. Think about it: For people who have never known a sunrise without advantage, losing a morsel of white privilege, real or imagined, is tantamount to losing ground.

A black pres-o-dent! My Gawd! The sky is falling!

Consider whites in the Deep South, where I live, who have still not gotten over the loss of the Civil War. Imagine what it feels like for them, slouched forlornly on plaid furniture, staring vacantly at TV sets, which force-feed them a daily dose of Obama-mania: "Barack Obama declared today…" or "Barack Obama signed a new law..." And worse, "President Obama traveled to Chicago on Air Force One…"

For me, there is a certain poetic justice in these anguished responses to progressive change. I must admit, I relish the idea of the progeny of whites who systematically erased blacks' African identity suddenly finding themselves subject to a president with a very African name. Barack Obama. Barack Obama. Barack Obama. This is pretty scary stuff, especially for the crowd that spends its days awaiting the eventual return of Elvis and Jesus, in that order. One can see them now, seething at the omnipresent media reminders of this seismic shift.

Barack Hussein Obama. The middle name especially effects a twist of the knife; it is akin to the grating sound of fingernails scraping a chalkboard. Trauma.

And why wouldn't there be trauma? This election not only made history. Perhaps more than any event in memory, Obama's victory has pried loose the stubborn grip of white supremacy. For many whites, it has crushed the essential foundation of their identities.

James Baldwin perhaps best captured what such a loss means to people who are taught from birth that white dominance is God ordained when he said,: "If I am not who you say I am, then that means you are not who you *think* you are."

So the deal is done. It's official: There's a brother in the White House, and he struts with a pimp. And untold numbers of white people in every corner of the country are confused, distraught, anxiety ridden. Where is Dr. Poussaint when we need him most?

A woman in Helena, Arkansas, told me that editors at the local newspaper were so disturbed by Obama's victory that they virtually ignored the historic occasion in print.

One is tempted to ask, why are these people still so implacable? Why have they been unwilling to accept their nation's electoral verdict?

They're pissed off because they now have to do what I have done all my life, which is comply with the directives of a national leader who does not look like me. White men in particular seem filled with inconsolable rage. For them, this election has served notice of a profound paradigm shift. John Wayne and Ronald Reagan are where they need to be: dead. As well, the pseudo-macho-manhood model they represent are graveyard bound.

Moreover, some people are resentful of Obama's victory simply because for the first time since they drew first breath they actually have to *think* about what it means to be white. Damn.

With the power of the ballot, a black man sleeps, eats—and makes love!—in the White House now. A black man with a chocolate wife and two beautiful children reside at 1600 Pennsylvania Ave. And get this: White people's tax dollars help pay the rent.

To their credit, many progressive white Americans are counted among those who helped nudge this country forward from the psychic gridlock that has stained its soul. As part of a broad coalition that transcended race, gender, class, sexual orientation, and even the generational divide, millions of whites sifted through deep-seeded fears and suspicions, stepped out of their racial comfort zones and took an electoral leap of faith.

That's the good news. On the other hand, it appears that whole coalition thing left many of us so excited that we've ignored the dangerously depressed state of our fellow citizens who preferred the status quo. And some of us have gotten so carried away as to suggest that the Obama victory has ushered in a new "post-racial" America.

Post-racial? In the words of the renowned armchair sage, Bill Cosby, "Come on, people." Granted, the jubilance of the moment is well-deserved. But let's not allow it to lead us back down the road to willful blindness and revisionist history. Before assembling a rainbow choir for a fresh rendition of Kumbaya, let us do a reality check.

The truth is, for all the glorious wonder of Obama's electoral win, we were *not* brought to this place by progressive thinking alone. In fact, this election was a nail biter that really should have been a stroll in the park.

In this election, Barack Obama, as brilliant a young mind as this country has produced, was pitted against Senator John McCain, once a decorated war hero, now stale white bread. It was so apparent during the presidential debates that Obama's progressive ideas and critical thinking skills were superior to those of McCain that it was insulting at times pretending it was an equal match. It was a bit like watching Muhammed Ali pummel some lightweight journeyman boxer in the ring, only to hear that the judges have scored the fight a dead heat heading into the final round.

Next, let's consider the stern resistance of many whites to Obama, a choice that really should have been a no-brainer from the start. One would think he would have been awarded the office on the basis of his proven ability to scale insurmountable odds. In order for Obama to get to this place, all the planets in the universe had to be rightly aligned; all conditions had to accommodate America's pathetically low threshold for racial tolerance.

Among them were at least four daunting requirements that bedeviled black presidential contenders that have come before:

1. Obama had to be someone whose white ancestry was not implicit, but visible;
2. He had to be a U.S. citizen whose background revealed no black ancestry traceable to guilt-inducing slavery;
3. He had to be a non-threatening black man (an oxymoron if ever there was one);
4. As much as is possible, he had to be nonracial.

To number one, Obama answered with a white mother; to number two, he claimed a Kenyan father; to numbers three and four, he performed a delicate racial high wire act that left much of the country amazed.

Dig this: He survived the standard slippery "Farrakhan-is-evil" attacks, with Jeremiah Wright as substitute; he outmaneuvered Hillary Clinton's aggressive gender ploy, which assumed a white woman was entitled to make presidential history first. (Hillary's sidekick proved that avowed southern racists such as David Duke pale compared to Geraldine Ferraro, the queen of self-righteous, indignant Yankees); Obama even out-foxed Slick Willie himself, Bill Clinton, who, thank God, finally was revealed to be a bootleg copy of a white liberal.

Still, Obama's brilliance, which inspired comparisons to the mythic "Camelot," seemed insufficient to win the trust and respect of whites in places such as Pennsylvania and Ohio. Such stubborn racial resistance brings to mind an observation Winston Churchill made about this country long ago: He said, "You can always count on Americans to do the right thing—*after* they have tried everything else."

Churchill was right. Obama's intellectual acuity, his tenacity and superb oratorical gifts demonstrated that he clearly was The Man. In so far as the condition of the country, all else had failed. To his credit, Obama repeatedly hammered that point home on the campaign trail. He reminded Americans that the country's monumental problems were generated by two disastrous terms of a white man, George W. Bush, whose stunning incompetence resulted in war and the worst economic crisis since the Great Depression.

With the very foundations of capitalism crumbling around them, some whites eventually put their racial attitudes aside in favor of self interest. Still, millions of others held fast, and even resorted to the sudden delusional embrace of a flighty former Alaskan beauty queen. This is the stuff that should fill therapists' couches.: To cross the racial divide at the polls, many white holdouts likely had to tap into a common neurosis, usually employed when they encounter black intelligence: They likely reassured themselves that the phenomenon that is Barack Obama was an exception, not the rule. That's it! Only *this* black man—the one with the white mama—can lead this great nation.

The reality is, Barack Obama is not the first Barack Obama. Over the centuries, this country has willfully forfeited valuable contributions from untold numbers of black geniuses, male and female, who were routinely passed over for mediocre whites. This is simply the first time America has been willing—Churchill might say, forced—to consider the best choice, regardless of race.

Post-racial? As one white man so aptly stated after the election, "It's hard for me to decide if we should be happy because this moment came so soon, or upset that it took so long."

With 69 million votes, Obama won, yes. Still, McCain racked up 59 million votes. The fact that the election was *that* close (nearly 53 percent for Obama, compared to almost 46 percent for McCain) is testament, it seems, to white America's reluctance to let go of the past. I say this, not to rain on this historic milestone, but to give voice to a reality that is conveniently being pushed aside. If nothing else, this election shook this country to its collective roots. It forced us to grapple more deeply with who we are as a nation, versus who we prefer to *think* we are.

It is safe to say, we still don't know.

So history has been made. Now to get on with its writing. The question is, how will President Obama do? Or better still, how will America do with him in office?

One is tempted to assume the numbers of traumatized whites will decline once the president proves that a black can run the country as effectively as those white men believed to have leadership embedded in their DNA.

I happen to disagree with the notion that Obama needs to prove himself to whites. Historically, white people's perceptions of blacks have been based less on facts than on lies, manufactured to justify slavery. They believed what they needed to believe, and for many, that need remains, though slavery is long dead.

Chief among the Obama-haters is radio talk show host Rush Limbaugh, who flat-out declared, "I hope he fails!"

Such comments demonstrate that, as with all things racial, this could turn ugly, fast. Blacks, extremely protective of Obama, are hypersensitive to unwarranted attacks. If they perceive that whites are applying a double standard or are less patient with him than they were with his reckless predecessor, Obama will serve as a lightning rod for racial strife, rather than the spark for reconciliation he aspires to be.

That seems likely, given that many whites insist they won't—indeed, they *can't*—take this election loss lying down; Limbaugh, the de facto leader of white extremism, rails so violently against President Obama that it appears sometimes that he might just blow a gasket. And while he bloviates on the airwaves, other fruitcakes spend their time crouched in dusty archive rooms, poring over Obama's birth certificate, hoping to find proof that our president is not a U.S. citizen.

You wonder, how does President Obama feel about all the venom directed his way. If it bothers him, he's not saying. He goes on, day by day, flashing that broad, effervescent smile. It brings to mind the cagey smile of Jack Johnson, America's first black heavyweight champ. Like Johnson, Obama's smile seems to conceal a taunting laughter beneath the surface. Johnson delighted in grinning at jeering Caucasian spectators as he vanquished white opponents, left and right.

Like Johnson, Obama smiles a lot, too, especially as he goes about appointing people of color to high positions; especially as he dismantles virtually every bad policy Bush and Dick Cheney put in place.

There is one comparison that many Obama supporters prefer not to think about. Johnson lived under the constant threat of death at the hands of racist whites. So, too, does Obama. At the start of the campaign, he received so many death threats that he was the first candidate in the race to receive secret service protection. Now that he is president, the stakes are raised. Given the history of racist violence that has nearly eviscerated black leadership it's no wonder that African Americans are praying, collectively holding their breaths. And given the white trauma that flourishes, every bit of that fear is justified.

Post racial? Someone should tell that to the crackpot Republican politician circulating "Barack the Magic Negro" DVD's from Tennessee.

All this madness and trauma led one progressive white man to write an article in a Macon, Georgia, newspaper, asking, "When are we white people going to get over it?"

He must know what a tall challenge he raised. We're talking about people whose minds are conditioned by a steady drumbeat of myths about great pale founding fathers. We're talking about a nation that has invested centuries in solidly constructing white privilege. It would be a mistake to think it will be de-constructed in one, or even two presidential terms.

So to the question, "When will whites get over it?" When one considers white trauma, the answer is clear: Not likely soon.

As for the rest of us, perhaps there is one small contribution we can make to the healing of America. When you run across one of the newly traumatized, offer them your place on the couch.

TONY MEDINA

Basketball Jones: Bofwana's Revenge (excerpt)

*Note from Tony: Obama goes to his left when the other team wants to force him to go right but then they ain't never played no ball like this with a baller like this on a court like this with the people in the stands like this waiting on the shots and the slams like this.

The sky opened up and clouds started marinating just above our heads. We thought it was about to rain, because all of a sudden it got real dark and the wind started whipping around 6th Avenue as if a tsunami was about to pimp smack its way through from the sweltering sewers of what we knew as Babylon. Lightening flashed on and off like a disco ball at The Latin Quarters or the Sound Factory. Thunder started clapping so fierce we thought Tito Puente, Eddie Palmieri, Celia Cruz, and Héctor LaVoe was about to descend from the heavens, singing, "Che-Che Che-Che Colé."

They unleashed their *secret* secret weapon on us: Katrina Bofwana. She was so hard everyone just called her by her last name like they do in the Army. Bofwana was light, bright, and full of fright. She was like Gorilla Monsoon, only she had a blond Mohawk weave with purple beaded plaits that hung down below her chin with its Kurt Douglas cleft. Her beaded braids would clank against her doorknocker earrings, making cowbell sounds when she dribbled the ball or checked you.

Like a fool, Chester Cheesecake hacked Bofwana so hard one of her breasts got loose from her bra and started rolling around all over the place, anchoring her in place. Now why did he go and do that? Normally, Bofwana would've chalked it up to another mug trying to cop a cheap feel. But with this hack she read hostility into it. All her eyes and flaring nostrils said was—*Oh, no you didn't!*

If this were a movie it would've been titled *Bofwana's Revenge*, starring Bofwana pimp smacking mugs all over the place, going to the hoop unchallenged.

She was so mad the hairs under her arms snarled at you, saying, *So what's up?* She turned into the Incredible Hulk right before our eyes. But since she was light skinned she didn't turn green, she just got red as the devil on a Louisiana Hot Sauce bottle.

This was the year of the first Black President. A b-baller and Hip Hop head who made his bones on the South Side of Chicago. Much to be admired. Much to be proud of. Everybody was walking around with Obama T-shirts. Everybody wanted change and peace in the world. Bofwana had an Obama shirt on but a pint-sized, clumsy-ass fool who had been named after his mama had an orgasm when she ate some cheesecake from a famous restaurant in Brooklyn, forced one of her big oblong papayas out of it. Everyone had peeped out one of Bofwana's John Cougar Melloncamps, and she was embarrassed and mad as all hell.

Her peoples started riding Chester Cheesecake, calling him Chester the Molester. Bofwana twisted Chester Cheesecake into some type of pretzel and hurled his ass over the fence of the Cage, and he went rolling up 6th Avenue beating all the yellow cabs and uptown buses back to Harlem.

Bofwana fouled out and we got to go to the free throw line. A riot nearly broke out when she got bumped, but the refs kept blowing their whistles until the crowd calmed down. The tension was so thick in the air you could cut it like a cheesecake.

Bro Ham Pete came in for Chester Cheesecake, a.k.a Chester the Molester, a.k.a the Rolling Pretzel of Harlem. He kept throwing up bricks and was sweating buckets till he had high water marks on his chin. Then a strong-ass extra strength breeze smacked its way through the court, making the peach fuzz on his goatee grow stalactites. The wind was so brutal it housed the ball, intercepting it in midair as it was about to clear net with a swish and loop-di-looped it cross court for an improbable bank shot, robbing Bro Ham Pete of his first ever free throw.

By this time, we sensed the game was cursed. We had to go deep into our arsenal and pull out somebody who had some serious mystical powers with him. Someone who smelled like he lived in a Botanica. We had to bring in Babalao Louie.

He always laughed at his grandmother whenever she got into her Santeria rituals, lighting candles and praying to the saints on her altar. This time he was a believer. He knew ornery spirits of bygone players who never made it pass their Rucker Park glory days and, reps falling to needles or prison or bullets or babies, haunted his chances of a title.

Matter of fact, there's a symbolic altar with white flowers and florida water on the court where one of our Old School ballers was shot. Our crew was adamant about it not being disturbed. Not to mention our framed picture of our idol, Earl "The Goat" Manigault (The Greatest of All Time, rest in peace), surrounded by white carnations floating in a bowl of holy water.

Babalao Louie, all dressed in white (from his headband to his Nikes), went up to the free throw line with all the swag of someone who'd spoken with the ancestors on a regular. Like he was Moses chillin' with a 40 at the Burning Bush. He prayed to Elegguá, St. Anthony, Oggún, Oshún, Changó, Obatalá. A mouth full of *bendiciones* to Shiva, Vishnu. A couple of Hail Marys. A forty-ounce tear bounce of Hosannas for the brothers who aren't here—trying not to throw up bricks. But nothing seemed to stick. If it didn't hit the backboard with such force it nearly shattered the glass like an Ella Fitzgerald note, it died in the air like a bird with Avian flu choking on some Avenue of the Americas smog.

Then Kiko Calabrizi, Chu Chu Valdez, and Iceberg Slim rushed Babalao Louie as he tried to recover his own rebound. Blahzay Dontay Alize Comprehenday got the loose ball, saved it from going out of bounds, and flung it to Chuletas who was making like he was painting his nails a fluorescent green. When Babalao Louie tried to grab the ball away, Chuletas put his hand up like Diana Ross singing, "Stop in the name of love," and said to him, "Get ye behind me, Satan! Talk to the hand!" Babalao Louie tried to roll around him, but Chuletas bumped him with his hipbone and kneed him in the nut sacks, making him see stars without the spangled banner. Babalao Louie stumbled around in a circle like Michael Spinks, saying "Tah-ee-ee-ee." Then asked the ref if he could pick up his nuts. The ref blew the whistle and gave him a penalty for insolence.

We got a little lucky when Yeah Yo went up to block a ball, stretching and straining so high up he not only almost got caught in a tree, he came down clutching his gut. It turned out he ate some mad greasy-ass leftovers minutes before the game and began crampin' up like he either had a period or was about to give birth right there on the court. It turned out Yeah Yo got the *churras*. That's the runs, i.e. he shit his drawers. He had the dire of the rears. And since he had on basketball trunks it dribbled down his leg like hot fudge on the side of a sundae. He was so tall it was like lava from Mount Vesuvius coming down hot and heavy and slow, threatening to take us all out.

My man Dunkin Donuts got the ball. When he went up for a lay-up a couple of Jehovah's Witnesses were trying to hand him an *Awake!,* and a Fruit of Islam cat in a bow tie was trying to sell him a bean pie and a *Final Call.* But he didn't let that disturb his groove. He whipped out a set of propellers and stuck it on his back and within seconds launched himself to the stratosphere of planet Dunky Dunk Dunk. Only he shot his wad too strong and wound up torpedoing himself head first into the hoop, his locks all tangled up in the gnarl and snake of the net.

A couple of the Young Sleazies started showboating with one another. Young Fo' Sheezy came out rockin' a crackberry like he was Russell Simmons or P. Diddy, followed by Young Phat Chance who was also stylin' some fancy pimped-out cell phone. Young Fo' Sheezy sent Young Phat Chance a text message as he approached the hoop. You would think he worked on Wall Street. He could answer his text messages in midair, with arm outstretched and ball rolling off his fingertips like a teardrop. He had a special technique that everyone tried to cop. Kind of like back when Grandmaster Flash started scratching on vinyl. He'd flick his wrist so fast, as if he were a magician trying to undress a set table by yanking the table cloth, leaving all the dishes and silverware intact. That was his go-to signature move like Jordan with his tongue hanging out. He flicked his wrist so many times he got carpal tunnel. Had to wear a special brace on his hand. It was with that brace he held a compact mirror so he could watch how fly he was whenever he went up for a lay-up. "You think my 'fro bounces too much when I go up?" he'd ask. His vanity knew no bounds. "You like the way the wind parts my 'fro?"

We were waiting for Sand Man from the Apollo to yank his ass off the court. Young Fo' Sheezy kept hogging the ball. He was such a ball fiend—afflicted with a basketball jones—we were going to have a drug intervention at the free throw line, but instead wheeled in Cochino Royale. He rode in on a bus from Our Lady of the Hairy Hangovers Church. His 'fro could be bent and twisted into all types of geometric shapes. He changed it up for damn near every other play. He wanted his hair to keep morphing geometric shapes, creating hybrids in order to cause the other team confusion. This go round he rocked an isosceles trapezoid and hung

Christmas ornaments off the tips that were turned upward like bullhorns. Then he freaked everybody out by changing it in midstream to antlers so he could make like Rudolph the Red Nose Reindeer. But it was the middle of July. I guess if we were in Puerto Rico or the D.R. or any old island, it wouldn't matter. But we were in the Village, in the butt crack of a sweltering morning, and he wanted everyone to call him Rudolph.

They brought in Chitlin Circuitbreaker, with his Mad Max thuggish ways. He was your garden-variety psychopath. Played ball on Ya Ba, some Thai meth he copped from a storefront in Astoria. Some secret underground Masonic Grand Poobah type shit. A real spoiled stingy paranoid dude. He was breastfed until he was eight. He was always drenched in sweat. The hairs on his arms and back were like concertina razor wire. He purposely brushed up against you when you checked him. It was like getting tazered. You had to use a cattle prod to keep from getting electrocuted by his ass. But that wasn't the half of it. The messed up part was that he had this long, droopy jheri curl that was so drenched in jheri curl juice his hair looked like an upside down Christmas tree dipped in motor oil and formaldehyde. It moved about the court like an octopus. Everybody started slipping and sliding and colliding into one another like we were the Keystone Cops.

They kept saying, "Yo, you be hackin'," and we'd say, "Nah, you be hawkin'!" This went on for quite sometime like an Abbot & Costello routine, until things began to get buck. They had on brass knuckles and carried bicycle chains. We had to break out our Bruce Lee nunchucks.

For some reason the older cats on the sidelines were chanting, "Everybody Wang Chung tonight." Then they broke out into "The Skeet National Anthem," singing, "Oh skeet skeet skeet skeet skeet skeet. Oh skeet skeet skeet skeet."

These cats were right out of Spofford in the Bronx. One of them was Nicky Barnes' daughter. You didn't fuck with her. Just gave her a free pass to the hoop.

We didn't have any Horatio Algers-type hoop dreams. We just had a day-to-day scheme of wanting to win the game this day. Being the baddest mofos on our block, in the city.; Harlem Globetrotter type shit. So we plowed through their sudden thuggish turn toward roughhouse brutality and commenced to do what we do best—run the court, pass, and dunk.

But every time I tried to get a cross-court pass, the ball would get sucked up into Chu Chu Valdez's 'fro like it was the Bermuda Triangle. His 'fro had a life of its own; it covered so much court. It was like a vacuum cleaner. Then the little Tattoo cat would emerge from Chu Chu's 'fro and, with ball in hand, slam-dunk it to spite us.

They were stylin' out about that dunk. So we had to get buck wild and threw them a couple of boomerang elbows and broke out in an electric boogaloo as we broke a nose or two to camouflage our foul shit for the refs. Mofos going for lay-ups in mid-court, seeing stars and shit. Everybody on the sidelines bustin' a gut, laughing at these silly-ass clusterfuck of clowns in the middle of the court, dizzy as shit, swatting flies.

Then they sent out Bumpy Johnson's great great grandson and that was all she wrote for that quarter. Nobody wanted to check that little ass tyrannical, Napoleonic sociopath. He had a fat dookey rope gold chain with an Oozy dangling from it. Fully locked and loaded and ready to bang. We had to carry that mug to the basket. We had to carry nunchucks and tazer guns just to check him.

By the time the fourth quarter started, my asthma started acting up. It didn't help much when they sent in their version of Cleopatra. At this point the Cage took on Biblical proportions. The court was like the Red Sea and who came out next was like the Burning Bush without Moses. My lungs nearly collapsed when China Roth seemed to glide to the court on one of them Spike Lee joint dollies, floating through everybody's heart, puttin' a hurtin' on our woody allens.

China Roth was Chinese, Jewish, and Black, in that order. She wore extensions in her hair so long they looked like a wedding gown train. When she entered the Cage it was like she was walking the red carpet at the Oscars or Grammys. She had her own paparazzi following her around like flies. They kept clicking off disposable cameras they got on sale at the Walmart or CVS. Her website simply said: *CHINA* in big bold letters that were trimmed in gold and encrusted with diamonds. When you clicked on it, you peeped a flash of her ass stuffed in pum-pum shorts and you heard her say, "Kiss my ass, biatch!" Her site had mad hits; it put Myspace and Facebook to shame. Everything she did was Youtubable. When you Googled her name, you didn't get anything about the country, but about how to get horse hair weaves and Lee Press-On Nails like China Roth. With the hundreds and thousands of daily hits you would think her hair and nails were Viagara and penis enlargement adds.

She rolled with Juebos Rancheros. Together they were like Bonnie & Clyde, Jay-Z & Beyonce. They had a serious running game that was hard to keep up with, especially when China Roth's wedding gown train of a weave obstructed your movement, hemming you up in the backcourt. But her man Juebos was ruthless to her Chaka Khan. He brought his Siberian huskies to the Cage and had to shave them down by the second quarter because it was the middle of July and the sun was blazin'. Juebos was part of a Black Bourgeois Yiddish glee club called The Oy Vey Beaujole. He was so closely associated with China Roth he had a conk and some Lee Press-On Nails, his damn self. And even though the look was a little suspect, he still got his thuggish swirl on on the court. They brought him and China Roth out to give Bofwana a hand and help fortify the game for them in the fourth quarter.

EDWARD S. SPRIGGS

The veil falls (Outside the womb)

i.

You came amid wraparound pages
Of election loony tunes
We returned innocently, chained
To TV blenders and the moneylenders
Our dreams still scattered everywhere
Still seeking nothing but our fair share

ii.

Now here you come.   You could be a pig in the poke
With that polished putty patina of global gluttony
Here you come in this magic millennium
Yet another middleman?
Another Harvard harlequin?
With our belts tightened to our core
We wondered if we could take it any more

iii.

Now here you come, a juggler man
Grinning tall in the Diaspora doors of dreams
Balancing promises of subprime notes
On the dirty confetti of Wall Street schemes
We knew a man was nothing but a man
Still you got our precious pent up votes
You rocked us wirelessly with "Yes We Can."

FARAI CHIDEYA

Educational Opportunity in the Age of Obama

In New York City on the sixteenth of July, the first black President of the United States looked out over a crowd gathered to celebrate the 100th anniversary of the NAACP. "There's a reason the story of the civil rights movement was written in our schools," President Obama said. "There's a reason Thurgood Marshall took up the cause of Linda Brown. There's a reason the Little Rock Nine defied a governor and a mob. It's because there is no stronger weapon against inequality and no better path to opportunity than an education that can unlock a child's God-given potential."

But the President went on to acknowledge that this was not a moment of unequivocal victory.

> [M]ore than a half century after Brown v. Board of Education, the dream of a world-class education is still being deferred all across this country. African-American students are lagging behind white classmates in reading and math–an achievement gap that is growing in states that once led the way on civil rights. Over half of all African-American students are dropping out of school in some places. There are overcrowded classrooms, crumbling schools, and corridors of shame in America filled with poor children – black, brown, and white alike.

In my time as a reporter and simply a citizen of the United States (one who went to public schools), I've seen communities deal with the two separate goals of educational equality and school integration. If a school is excellent but all non-white, is that the vision of Brown achieved? What if it is integrated, but mediocre or worse? Unfortunately, I've seen too many schools where neither the goals of integration nor excellence were met. While writing the 1999 book *The Color of Our Future*, I visited many schools which were what I call "ABW"—black, Latino, Asian, Native

American—anything but white. The students often struggled to get basic supplies, qualified teachers, and adequate space.

The Media Academy at Fremont High School in Oakland put those struggles in plain sight. It lies on a street filled with idling day laborers, and operates out of worn trailers or "portables" over a decade old,. but it has a track record of doing big things with tough or educationally challenged kids.

Earlier this year, I brought graduate students from the journalism school at The University of California, Berkeley, to meet the teens at Fremont High. The grad students were a mix of races, themselves, but the Fremont students were immigrants from several countries including Vietnam and El Salvador as well as black students born in the neighborhood. As was true a decade ago, the high school was what I call "ABW"—Anything But White.

We talked about media, education funding cuts and local school closures (which one brave Fremont student was investigating, much to the consternation of some officials), plus issues including the economy and the fatal shooting of a cuffed man by transit police on New Year's day. A mix of student and professional crews videotaped the event so we could leave some record of who we were and what we are struggling with in our time.

In another environment, many of these kids would be tracked low-achieving or low-literacy and put on the back burner of society. Instead, this graduation season brings moments of joy as students from this tough little program get their diplomas and gear up to go to college. Thisat kind of scene doesn't happen often enough.

Yes, the Obama Administration is juggling the crises of jobs, foreclosures, banking, wars, and healthcare. We still have to ask when our President intends to foreground educational opportunity, and what he will ask of us as a nation. For example: how will we balance short-term stopgapping with "big think" long-term change? Why are so many public schools today, even high-achieving ones, "ABW"? Is school integration effectively dead, fifty-five years after *Brown v. Board of Education*? How can not just white but middle—and upper-middle—income families be reconnected to public schooling? Will the new political rainbow coalition lose its might once people start debating who should get affirmative action–rich and black, or poor and white? Will "equality," in this economic crisis, mean that more white Americans are poorly educated, as opposed to more students of color doing well? (That prospect should chill our bones.)

There are moments in education where the promise is fulfilled, ... where racial integration meets excellence. I was privieleged to see one of them via the lens of my family.

My cousin Adia was one of men and women I saw graduate from Morehouse Medical School in the spring of 2009. The school is affiliated with Morehouse College, the historically black male undergraduate institution founded after the Civil War. Yet though the majority of students and families were black American, other families helping to robe the newly-minted doctors included women in saris or wearing Muslim headscarves; mothers and fathers in lavish matching garb from West Africa; parents with the last name Chen or Rodriguez; and families from our nation's racial majority for another three decades, plus or minus: white Americans.

Just a decade ago, America was in denial about our rapidly changing racial and cultural landscape. The U.S. Census had released projections that by the year 2050, America would have no racial majority. Today, they've moved that projected date up to 2042.

Some people think that having a black President means we can afford to put away the topic of race altogether. That complacency, combined with our current economic crisis, could put the lives and futures of students at risk. Education is what turns the American Dream into the American Reality. And education is in deep trouble, first as a thing-in-itself, and also as an indicator of our racial future.

During his speech to the NAACP, the President mixed critique of parents and society with an exhortation to increase expectations:

"[Success] means pushing our kids to set their sights higher. They might think they've got a pretty good jump shot or a pretty good flow, but our kids can't all aspire to be the next LeBron or Lil Wayne. I want them aspiring to be scientists and engineers, doctors and teachers, not just ballers and rappers. I want them aspiring to be a Supreme Court Justice. I want them aspiring to be President of the United States."

That's an admirable sentiment. But how do we achieve it? No black-tie-dinner speech can allow enough time to outline policy objectives. But our financial crisis seems to have slowed the Administration's attention to education just as education in America is weakened by the erosion of the tax base.

The election of Barack Obama, the centennial of the NAACP, and the increasing racial diversity of the nation show that we are making some steady progress towards racial equality. But we must make space at the crowded table of public policy agendas for education. Regarding education, we must decide if we want school integration, top-notch quality, or both—and what we are willing to do to achieve those goals.

Auto-correcting History

—for President Barack Obama

Spell check does not recognize
this name –yet.

It tries, with a red underline alert,
to tell me that this is wrong,
that my letters are misplaced,
leading my complicated PC,
with its perfect vocabulary,
to believe no such same name exists.

It offers suggestions to fix
what history has already confirmed.

These letters, round-about, with all
their beautiful curves and angles,
their intricate folds forming perfect B's
and A's and the roundest O,
shaping a name that has awakened us all.

Barack and Obama cause key stroke duels
between my auto-correct and me.
Not willing to give up,
it plugs in Brick and Abeam, trying to
hold on tight to its King's English.

This name isn't a mistake.
No slip of the keys on my part.
No half asleep or dazed typing.
No hurry rush of tidal wave words and wonder.

Every letter in this name comes with purpose.
Each key stroke is meant.
I highlight the name, click "add to dictionary."
I auto-correct my spell check.

It must be understood that he exists,
that we exist.

We are real and breathing.

MICHAEL SIMANGA

First President and First Lady
January 20, 2009

On a cold January night
the beginning of a long
new day
we watched them dance
deep inside a
sweet soul music trance
her head on his shoulder
his hand on her back
moving
to a promise
to love
each other
and us

QUINCY TROUPE

Three Editorials

(From *Black Renaissance Noire*)

A note on the three editorials

These three editorials were written over a span of a year, from February 2008 until February 2009, when the last one was written. They were penned for Black Renaissance Noire, a literary, academic, art, cultural, and social journal that I edit for the Institute of African-American Affairs at New York University in New York City.

After I had retired from teaching at the University of California, San Diego, and returned to Harlem, New York, where I had lived previously for 20 years, I was invited to become editor of the journal in the Fall of 2004 by the founding editors: Manthia Diawara, director of the Institute of African-American Affairs; Dr. Clyde Taylor, recently retired professor from New York University; and Walter Mosley, novelist.

The first two editorials remain pretty much intact, though I have deleted material that addressed who was being published in each of those issues. On the other hand, I have expanded substantially the contents and focus of the third editorial for publication in this anthology. While all of these editorials deal directly with the candidacy of Barack Obama in his run for the presidency and the possibility of his election to that office, I felt it was necessary to include my thoughts on his historic election as the first recognizable African American to the office of President of the United States in the third editorial.

Despite our personal achievements and collective contributions in elevating the United States as great and respected nation around the world, Obama's presidency represents a significant step forward in a long, tortured, glorious journey for African-Americans to gain their full rights in this country. The journey has not ended. Barack Obama's ascendancy to the presidency is just another giant step up the ladder in achieving full equality for all African-Americans.

Winter/Spring, 2008 Editorial for *Black Renaissance Noire*

The year 2008 might prove to be one of the most pivotal years in the history of the United States, and indeed of the entire world, in a very long time. For starters, after forty-nine years in power, Cuban president Fidel Castro has relinquished his position as head of state. The wars in Afghanistan and Iraq, as well as the Israeli/Palestinian conflict, continue to fester, causing massive tensions and disruptions in relations between Western and Middle Eastern nations. The assassination of Benazir Bhutto in Pakistan late last year has that nation reeling, costing that country's former strongman, Pervez Musharraf, his majority in parliament in a nation where the Taliban and Osama Bin Laden remain constant thorns in the side of American regional foreign policy goals. The African continent remains rife with debilitating, bloody ethnic and tribal conflicts, with Kenya and the Democratic Republic of the Congo (formerly Zaire) being prime examples of this chaos, while Ghana, South Africa, Uganda, Rwanda, Mali, Senegal, Benin, Tanzania, Namibia, and others remain relatively stable and peaceful.

President George W. Bush is in the final phase of his ruinous eight-year reign in office, one that has been filled with incredibly hardheaded, boneheaded decisions including the war in Iraq that has cost taxpayers billions of dollars and killed, wounded, and displaced millions of Iraqi citizens and American soldiers, as well as the U.S. homeowners sub-prime banking loan mortgage crisis that has lost so many—and especially African-Americans—their homes. Failed foreign and domestic policies abound everywhere we look. Bush's presidency has been filled with widespread "bumpkinology" (my neologism for Bush's incompetence), corruption, and cronyism, resulting in one of the largest transferals of wealth (taxpayers' money to corporations) in the history of the nation through no-bid contracts under the rubric of the war in Iraq, and the giveaways of vast sums of money to Republican friends charged with rebuilding New Orleans and the Gulf Coast of Mississippi in the aftermath of Hurricane Katrina.

The gross incompetence of Bush's two-term reign as president would be comic were it not so calamitous in its execution of domestic, financial, and foreign policies—with his AIDS program in Africa being possibly one notable exception. Taken as a whole, however, the last eight years of the Bush administration is nothing to laugh about, not least because the United States has suffered incredible long-standing blows to its prestige and standing throughout the world. It appears, however, that a silver lining may be hidden in the disastrous legacy of the Bush administration.

Which brings me to the meteoric political rise of Senator Barack Obama of Illinois in his race to become the Democratic Party nominee in the 2008 race for the presidency of the United States. At the time of this writing, Senator Obama has waged a brilliant campaign, winning twelve straight Democratic presidential primaries and caucuses, and soundly defeating the seven other contenders in the process, including (so far) former first lady and New York senator Hillary Clinton. It is astonishing how quickly Senator Obama has exploded onto the American and international political scene. For the first time in American history, an identifiable African American has gone this far in the race to become president of the United States, notwithstanding the longstanding rumors that at least five former U.S. presidents (i.e. Thomas Jefferson, Andrew Jackson, Abraham Lincoln, Warren Harding, and Calvin Coolidge) were blacks who passed for white. And while Jesse Jackson's candidacy was also historic, he never got as far as Barack Obama has in this election. In the unlikely event (given Obama's current lead in number of delegates and caucuses and primaries won) that Senator Hillary Rodham Clinton becomes the Democratic Party nominee in the 2008 presidential contest, this election year will still have been historic. It will be the first time that a woman and a recognizable African descendant have come this far in the race for this nation's highest office.

I predict that Senator Barack Obama will, in fact, become the Democratic candidate for president, go on to defeat the Republican nominee, Senator John McCain from Arizona, and eventually win this nation's highest office in November. All this despite the widespread media bias, so evident only three days before the March 4 primaries, especially from prominent cable anchors like Wolf Blitzer of CNN, MSNBC's Joe Scarborough and Chris Matthews, and conservative radio talk show host Rush Limbaugh, who admonished his listeners in Ohio, Texas, Vermont and Rhode Island to vote against Senator Obama in favor of Senator Clinton, after having her husband, former president Bill Clinton, on his show.

At the same time, we've never before had so many citizens—

especially people under the age of thirty—involved in the political process. The prospect that either a woman or an African American man will hold the country's highest office leaves us absolutely giddy. Whoever wins, the 2008 race for the presidency shows that the nation has made significant progress towards political maturity. On the other hand (and despite the reality of this feel-good moment), we must remember and forever be aware, if truth be told, that we still have a very long way to go as a nation in our struggle to achieve religious tolerance, social justice, gender equality, racial harmony, and a color- blind society.

Fall 2008 Editorial for *Black Renaissance Noire*

As this issue of *Black Renaissance Noire* is published, we, the American people, are debating for whom to cast our ballots in the historic 2008 presidential election. "Historic" because for the first time in this nation's long, tortured, and illustrious history, an African American, Barack Obama, has won the right to compete to lead our nation. In my last editorial, I predicted that Obama would not only defeat Hillary Rodham Clinton in his fight for the democratic nomination but would also go on to win the presidency in November in a head-to-head fight with John McCain. I stand by that prediction.

An Obama victory in November will bring about enormous change in this country; especially in the way Americans view each other. It will alter the way we Americans think about our future political leadership. That's a good thing, and it's about time this happens because in a multicultural, multiracial, multi-religious country like the one we live in, no single group should ever have total say over what is good or bad for this nation. Beyond my own personal prediction of an Obama victory, let me say this: whoever wins the presidency, this election has the capacity to heal our tortured nation or completely rip it asunder, and I say this with both a hopeful and a heavy heart.

Any way you slice it, change by its very nature is revolutionary, carrying both positive and dangerous elements within its transformational impulse. An example of modern-day change is how, in this age of the blogosphere and 24/7 cable networks, the "fleas on the dog," as *The New*

York Times put it when referring to print, electronic, and web journalists and cable news pundits who report and slant the news, have transformed how people receive and act on information. It is stunning how so many people get their information from websites rather than from print media, radio or television.

And so we will have to wait and see how the country reacts to the results of this cataclysmic election cycle: either we will go down a hopeful, healing road or we will travel a path fraught with a more virulent, destructive, and I believe, fascistic brand of racism. In my opinion, young voters hold the key to the way the nation goes in this very important electoral cycle.

If John McCain wins this presidential election, friends of mine— African American, white, Jewish, Latino, Asian, Arab, and Native American alike—see an America moving towards a future with Hitlerian tendencies. It is my fervent hope and wish, however, that such a scenario does not come to pass because what it portends for our already fragile democracy is too terrible to contemplate.

If the many far-right-wing white zealots we hear calling in on C-Span, talk radio and even some of the anchors and commentators on cable TV programs (who support a McCain-Palin presidency because they are terrified of the promise of an African American president) are any indication, we are witnessing a perilous moment in our nation's history. They prefer that the nation elect the dangerously erratic, impulsive, political "maverick" John McCain, whose hot temper and bad judgment have led him to select Sarah Palin; how else to explain his ridiculous choice of this clueless governor of Alaska, who is, in her own words, "a pit bull with lipstick," and an extremely radical right-wing, white, female ideologue, as his vice presidential running mate? This is nothing more than McCain's cynical ploy to appeal to his Christian white, right- wing base and to so-called "disaffected Hillary Clinton" white, middle-aged to older female and male voters. It is a sad spectacle to watch—not to mention having to listen to all of "McSane's" ridiculous lies—and very, very dangerous for the future of our country because neither McCain, nor Palin, has a vision for a rapidly changing domestic and international sphere. Still, McCain's cynical ploy could backfire and fail. Let's hope so.

Obama, on the other hand, while not a perfect candidate, does have a vision as to where this country has to go. Despite his flaws, he is an accomplished, brilliant thinker; a man whose progressive vision for our nation values the negotiation of problems and conflicts over a path that will ultimately lead us down a road of continuous death and war.

The situation would be laughable were it not so serious and deadly. If you look closely, most of these McCain supporters are the very same people who gave us the last disastrous eight years of George W. Bush and Dick Cheney. It's complete and utter madness to believe that any sane American would still want to believe in this absurd folly, but many do, especially a large percent of so-called blue-collar workers, values-issue people, and hockey moms: code names for racist white people, who can never, ever envision an African American as president. And that is what this election is all about, no matter the fact African Americans have always supported white candidates for office. And where were all the people of color at the 2008 Republican National Convention? In the final analysis, I am convinced, unfortunately, that Obama's chances narrow as this election threatens to be increasingly defined by fear and racial anxieties, not the important issues of the day.

It is time—past the time—for all fair-minded Americans to be vigilant, to pull our heads up out of the sand, pay close attention to what is really happening to our country, and finally, to keep up our guard to prevent the realization of such a terrible potential social and political development. Otherwise, a horrific reckoning awaits the American way of life and the "great experiment" in which many of us have participated and cherished will perish. Such a dark prognostication greatly saddens me, but I am convinced that our country is at a crossroads, at the edge of a Mount Everest-like fall, especially in the wake of the frightening Wall Street financial debacle and the subsequent tax payer-government sponsored bailout and takeover. Under this unprecedented plan, so-called ardent free-market capitalists, who have privatized tremendous profits, now will be allowed to socialize their risks and debts back to the average American taxpayers. What a system!

In March, when this issue of *Black Renaissance Noire* is published, Barack Hussein Obama will have been the 44th President of the United States for two months (I just love saying the words President Barack Obama.). His election to the office of President is still amazing to me. The night of his victory, November 4th, was an incredible evening of joy in Harlem, New York, where I live. People poured out into the streets celebrating President-elect Obama's victory.

The overwhelmingly positive energy of thousands of joyous, smiling faces of all ages, races, genders, sexual orientation, with tears flowing down their cheeks, was astonishing, beautiful and exalting, as were the celebrations in Chicago's Grant Park, Obama's adopted home, before he moved to the White House. It was something I thought I would never see in my lifetime, although like many other African Americans in this country, I had always hoped it would happen. This historic event triggered a similar outpouring of joy and celebration around the world.

His inauguration ceremony on January 20th, on the western front of the U.S. Capitol, facing the austere Washington Monument, in front of 2 million freezing, ecstatic people on a frigidly cold Sunday, was also an exhilarating occasion. To the relief of millions world-wide, President Obama's victory dropped the curtain on the ruinous, calamitous eight year, fear-filled reign of the "Boy King," President George W. Bush.

On the other hand, an Obama presidency also brings with it the expectation that this young, gifted president can guide the United States out of one of the most horrific financial, social and political periods in our history. Further, as a nation, we are faced with immense religious, social, cultural and political divisions that only exacerbate the dilemmas in which we find ourselves.

These problems sometimes seem intractable. Witness the contentious, acrimonious deadlock between Republicans and Democrats over the passage of the $787 billion dollar stimulus legislation signed in the first 30 days of President Obama's administration. Yet, no other president in recent memory accomplished so much during the first 40 days of his administration.

Obama signed the Lilly Ledbetter Fair Pay Restoration Act that extends the time to file suits claiming discrimination on the basis of sex, race or religion. He signed an executive order to close the gap in health insurance for young people; announced a date–August 2010–to end the war in Iraq; signed a $3.7 trillion dollar first term budget, that includes historic levels of funding for health care, retro-fitting and greening the nation, for increasing education, new energy initiatives, infrastructure funding for highways, mass transit and high speed trains, broadband internet infrastructure, the National Endowment for the Arts and the Humanities, tax hikes for the wealthy, and tax cuts for lower-income American citizens. In short, President Obama passed more legislation in 40 days than most other Presidents passed in one or two terms.

These initiatives and ideas simultaneously have caused joy, outrage and bewilderment. But in the sausage-making process of producing legislation, passing bills in Washington and throughout state and municipal governments all over the United States is an unsavory business. There is no way in this process to satisfy every body. Inherent in the necessity of compromise in order to fashion a broad-based consensus among political rivals unfailingly results in consternation on all sides and is a breeding ground for divisions.

Such divisions will continue to test the resolve of the American people to embrace President Obama's concept of change. Yet change is necessary, if the USA is to move forward and begin the task of transforming itself. It is also necessary if this country is to regain its status as a great and respected nation around the world. But, as we all know, change is "easier said than done" and has never been a concept easily embraced. Instead it has always been contentious and acrimonious (if and when achieved), and it will remain so today.

Witness the infamous cartoon depicting two white policemen shooting a monkey—a thinly disguised reference to President Obama—with one policemen uttering the words: "They'll have to find someone else to write the next stimulus bill," that appeared in the *New York Post* newspaper on February 18, 2009. Not only outrageous in its open racism, this cartoon advocates the assassination of the President of the United States, a crime of treason, punishable by death.

Add to this cartoon, the incident of the white Los Alamitos, California, mayor, Dean Grose, sending out an image with watermelons displayed on the lawn of the White House, suggesting that kids will have to participate in a watermelon roll rather than the traditional Easter egg hunt. The stupidity of the assumption that ALL African Americans love watermelon notwithstanding, this clumsy attempt at degrading African Americans and ridiculing Obama's presidency ignores the health benefits of this delicious fruit, especially vis-à-vis the cholesterol producing egg! Thankfully, the intellectually challenged California mayor resigned his office within days of his antic being broadcast in the media.

Despite the fact that President Obama inherited a host of very large problems exacerbated by the failed presidency of George W. Bush, the fact remains these problems are now President Obama's problems. It is now Obama's task to create and offer up a coherent, workable vision that will help provide solutions to the enormous challenges facing his presidency, if his presidency is to be judged a success. Whatever the future holds for this charismatic President, who is already showing a very bold, transforming, forward-looking vision and legislative agenda, Mr. Obama will still have to be held accountable for the successes and failures—let us hope his failures are few—of his administration.

As of this writing the Obama administration is still in flux. I am confident he will become a great president, though I believe he needs all concerned, conscious, progressive citizens to critique, criticize, and push him constantly—even when he might not WANT to be pushed—to remind him of the important promises he made as a candidate and must deliver over the next four years. For instance, what will he do about the nation's unjust justice system when it comes to dealing with its minority citizens, especially black and Latino men? What will be his policy on and relationship with Cuba, with African countries, Venezuela, the corrosive Israeli-Palestian conflict, conflicts in Afghanistan and Pakistan, our relationship with China, Europe, the Caribbean, Mexico, Central and Latin America?

Barack Obama is the President now—not a candidate for the office—and his most ardent supporters—I count myself in that group—including African-Americans will have to find ways to openly disagree with him when it is necessary. And these disagreements, like family arguments will bring tension to the relationship. This is to be expected. In the end, no matter how much African-Americans love, are proud of and respect President Obama, we must STILL hold him accountable—like any other American President—for what he does, or does not do for the country and for black communities across the nation.

Barack Obama is President because of the epic civil rights struggle of Fannie Lou Hammer; Ella Baker; Stokely Carmichael; the NAACP; SNCC; Dr. Martin Luther King and Malcolm X; Jesse Jackson and Reverend Al Sharpton, just to mention a few. The achievements of these Americans and the massive African-American voter turn-out (as well as the turn-out of people of all ages and races in the 2008 presidential election) helped to bring Barack Obama to the dance, to the presidential balls. It behooves us to remind our beloved Obama to remain conscious of this fact and hold his feet to the fire, albeit in the most constructive way and within the right context.

Some say he could be bolder and this might prove to be true. But let us not forget he is a black man, and we ALL know how many European-Americans react to a brilliant, confident, bold-thinking African-American male. They think he is uppity, arrogant, don't know his proper place even though he is the president. This is a problem for President Obama and will remain a problem—though it isn't his—and up until now President Obama has handled it adroitly.

Because he will make mistakes, he is not a savior, but he most definitely promises to be much better than what we have had in the past from this nation's Presidents, including Bill Clinton, adored by black people, but who allowed the massacre to happen in Rwanda. Bill Clinton seduced us with his saxophone and dark glasses, his visits to black churches, his love of gospels, barbeque ribs and collard greens.

The agenda put forth so far by President Barack Obama is ambitious, and it will be difficult—though not impossible—to accomplish. I am certain he will most likely succeed as president, because he is a brilliant, confident, strategic thinker—also patient—and has shown that he can be "cold-blooded" enough to do what is necessary to accomplish whatever he wants to get done. At the time of this writing, President Obama is tackling the immense housing problem, another challenge with collapsing banks, the looming bankruptcies of Detroit automakers, universal health care, wars in Iraq and Afghanistan, and on and on and on, ad infinitum.

So I wish him all the luck in his endeavors. I feel certain he will do all he can to provide solutions for the problems facing this nation and deliver us all "the change we need." Of this I am confident, especially if we deliver on our responsibility to be "good citizens," to do our part, hold his feet to the fire, and remain vocal against all those forces seeking to undermine his presidency with forceful, civic, political, and social activism. But he must be bold because he might not get but one swing at the presidential bat; he might not be re-elected for a second term, or (and I hate to bring this up) he could be assassinated by some crazed right-wing racist. After all, hate groups are on the rise exponentially in this country.

In the end I am confident he will do all that he can to deliver solutions this country so desperately needs. But to do this he needs to bring his A game to the presidential court everyday and I am certain he will do this. But we, too, as citizens, must remember the journey that brought all of US to this historic moment, and always act responsibly by bringing *our* A game to this remarkable, momentous moment.

Malaika Adero is Vice President and Senior Editor of the Simon and Schuster publishing imprint Atria Press. She is the author of *Up South: Stories, Studies and Letters of The Centuries African American Migration* and the co-author of *Speak, So You Can Speak Again: The Life of Zora Neale Hurston*. Adero is also a visual artist who uses mixed media, oils and photography. Her work has been shown at Corridor Gallery and The Gallery at Harriet's Alter Ego in Brooklyn, The Arts Students League in Manhattan and Indusa Gallery in Harlem.

Sababa Akili is a political activist, writer, creative and technical artist. sababa.akili@post.harvard.edu

Tina McElroy Ansa is a novelist, publisher, filmmaker, teacher and journalist. She grew up in Middle Georgia in the 1950s hearing her grandfather's stories on the porch of her family home and strangers' stories downtown in her father's juke joint, which have inspired Mulberry, Georgia, the mythical setting of her four novels, *Baby of the Family, Ugly Ways, The Hand I Fan With* and *You Know Better.* In 2005, Ms. Ansa was awarded the 2005 Stanley W. Lindberg Award for her work and contributions to the literary arts community of Georgia. In March 2007, Ms. Ansa launched an independent publishing company, DownSouth Press, which focuses on African-American fiction and nonfiction.

Amiri Baraka is the author of over 40 books of essays, poetry, drama, and music history and criticism. A poet icon and revolutionary political activist, his influences range from musical orishas such as Ornette Coleman, John Coltrane, Thelonius Monk, and Sun Ra to the Cuban Revolution, Malcolm X and world revolutionary movements. Baraka is renowned as the founder of the Black Arts Movement in Harlem in the 1960s that became, though short-lived, the virtual blueprint for a new American theater aesthetics. He has been the subject of numerous documentary films and his awards and honors include an Obie, the American Academy of Arts & Letters award, the James Weldon Johnson Medal for contributions to the arts, Rockefeller Foundation and National Endowment for the Arts grants, Professor Emeritus at the State university of New York at Stony Brook, and Poet Laureate of New Jersey.

Tara Betts is the author of *Arc & Hue*. Her work appears in several journals and anthologies, including *Gathering Ground*, *ROLE CALL*, and *Fingernails Across a Chalkboard*. She teaches creative writing at Rutgers University and is a Cave Canem Poetry Fellow. www.tarabetts.net

Antoinette Brim is the author of the poetry collection, *Psalm of the Sunflower* (Willow Books/Aquarius Press). She is a Cave Canem Poetry Fellow and a recipient of the Archie D. and Bertha H. Walker Foundation Scholarship to the Fine Arts Work Center in Provincetown. She earned an MFA in Creative Writing-Poetry from Antioch University, Los Angeles. www.antoinettebrim.com

Jericho Brown was the speechwriter for the Mayor of New Orleans before receiving his PhD in Creative Writing and Literature from the University of Houston. He also holds an MFA from the University of New Orleans and a BA from Dillard University. The recipient of the Whiting Writers Award, the Bunting Fellowship from the Radcliffe Institute at Harvard University, and two travel fellowships to the Krakow Poetry Seminar in Poland, Brown teaches creative writing as an assistant professor of English at the University of San Diego. His poems have appeared in *The Iowa Review*, *jubilat*, *New England Review*, *Oxford American*, and several other journals and anthologies. His first book, *PLEASE* (New Issues), won the 2009 American Book Award. www.jerichobrown.com

Farai Chideya is a broadcaster, author, and multi-media journalist. She is the founder and managing editor of PopandPolitics.com, a contributor at WNYC, and previously hosted the nationally syndicated African-American/African-diaspora program News and Notes for NPR. Her three non-fiction books include *Don't Believe the Hype: Fighting Cultural Misinformation About African-Americans* and *The Color of Her Future*. At the time of this book's publication, she is nominated for a 2010 NAACP Image Award for her novel *Kiss the Sky*. www.faraichideya.com

Pearl Cleage is an Atlanta-based writer whose works include seven novels, including *What Looks Like Crazy On An Ordinary Day*, and thirteen plays, including *Flyin' West* and *A Song for Coretta*. Her most recent novel, *Till You Hear From Me*, will be published by Ballantine/One World in April 2010. Her new play, *The Nacirema Society Requests the Honor of Your Presence at a Celebration of Their One Hundred Anniversary* was co-produced by The Alabama Shakespeare Festival and The Alliance Theatre in the Fall of 2010. Pearl is the wife of writer Zaron W. Burnett, Jr., with whom she often collaborates. www.PearlCleage.net

Chuck D is the founder of Public Enemy and one of the most colossal figures in the history of hip-hop, not to mention its most respected intellectual. He is extremely politically active as he has co-hosted *Unfiltered* on Air America Radio, testified before Congress in support of peer-to-peer MP3 sharing, and was involved in a 2004 rap political convention. He continues to be an activist, publisher, lecturer, and producer, as well as an in-demand speaker on the college lecture circuit.

Kwame Dawes was born in Ghana and was educated at Jamaica College, the University of the West Indies and the University of New Brunswick, where he gained his Ph.D. He is currently a professor of English and the Director of the S. C. Poetry Initiative at the University of South Carolina, where he has taught since 1992. A reviewer, broadcaster, actor, storyteller, broadcaster, critic, poet and playwright, Dawes is the programmer for the Calabash International Literary Festival held in St. Elizabeth, Jamaica, each year, and is the Director of the Calabash Writer's Workshop. His awards include The Forward Poetry Prize, the Hollis Summers Poetry Prize, a Pushcart Prize, and the Poetry Business Award.

LaTasha Diggs is a writer, vocalist, and sound artist in New York. She is the author of three chapbooks which include *Ichi-Ban and Ni-Ban* (MOH Press), and *Manuel is destroying my bathroom* (Belladonna Press), as well as the album, *Television*. Her work has been published in *Rattapallax*, *Black*

Renaissance Noir, Nocturnes, Drumvoices Review, The Black Scholar, P.M.S, and *Bum Rush the Page.* Diggs has received scholarships, residencies, and fellowships from Cave Canem, Harvestworks Digital Media Arts Center, Naropa Institute, Caldera Arts, and The New York Foundation for the Arts. www.latashadiggs.com

Kelly Norman Ellis is an associate professor of English and associate director of the MFA in Creative Writing program at Chicago State University. Her first collection of poetry entitled *Tougaloo Blues* was published by Third World Press and she is the co-editor of *Spaces Between Us: Poetry, Prose and Art on AIDS/HIV.* She is a Cave Canem Poetry Fellow and founding member of the Affrilachian Poets.

Martín Espada has published seventeen books as a poet, editor and translator. His collection of poems entitled *The Republic of Poetry* (Norton, 2006) received a Paterson Award for Sustained Literary Achievement and was a finalist for the Pulitzer Prize. He has received numerous fellowships and awards, including a Guggenheim Fellowship. Espada teaches at the University of Massachusetts-Amherst. www.martinespada.net

Ross Gay is the author of the poetry collection, *Against Which.* He teaches at Indiana University in Bloomington.

Keith Gilyard a native New Yorker, has lectured widely on language, literature, education, and civic affairs. His books include the education memoir *Voices of the Self: A Study of Language Competence* (1991*),* for which he received an American Book Award; *Let's Flip the Script, An African American Discourse on Language, Literature, and Learning* (1996); *Composition and Cornel West: Notes toward a Deep Democracy* (2008); and *John Oliver Killens: A Life of Black Literary Activism* (2010). He is currently Distinguished Professor of English at The Pennsylvania State University, University Park.

Jasmine Guy is an actress, writer, dancer, choreographer and director. A veteran of the Alvin Ailey Dance Company and well known for her role as

Whitley on the television show *A Different World* she has also appeared in a variety of films, television shows and stage productions. In addition to her other creative projects, she has focused her attention on directing and has staged several productions, including an innovative reimagining of the classic Ntozake Shange play, *for colored girls who have considered suicide when the rainbow is enuf.* She is the author of *Evolution of a Revolutionary,* the biography of Afeni Shakur, mother of the late artist Tupac Shakur.

Kevin Harewood is a native of the Bedford Stuyvesant section of Brooklyn, NY. An entertainment and media industry veteran, he has worked with the likes of Chris Rock, Martin Lawrence, Bill Nunn, Freddie Jackson, Gordon Chambers and others. His conviction about his inner-city community was showcased in his film, *25 Strong- A Film About Basketball! A Film About Life!* His EDclectic Entertainment firm is involved in the production of live performance events and independent films. www.edclecticentertainment.com

Lita Hooper is an associate professor of English at Georgia Perimeter College. She is the author of *Art of Work: The Art and Life of Haki Madhubuti* (2006) and *Thunder in Her Voice: The Narrative of Sojourner Truth* (2010). She earned an MA in Creative Writing from the University of Colorado (Boulder) and a DA from Clark Atlanta University. Her work has appeared in journals, magazines and anthologies. She is a Cave Canem Poetry Fellow and a recipient of several artist residencies/fellowships. www.litahooper.com.

Randall Horton is the author of the poetry collections The *Definition of Place,* and the *The Lingua Franca of Ninth Street,* both from Main Street Rag. He is the co-editor of *Fingernails Across the Chalkboard Poetry and Prose on HIV/AIDs from the Black Diaspora.* He has a MFA in poetry from Chicago State University and a PhD in English/Creative Writing from SUNY Albany. He teaches at the University of New Haven.

Gloria House is professor of Humanities and African American Studies at the University of Michigan, Dearborn, and Professor Emerita in the Interdisciplinary Studies Department of Wayne State University. Since the

1960s when she worked as a student in the Southern Civil Rights Movement, Dr. House has been an activist in African American community issues and Third World solidarity causes. Her publications include three poetry collections, *Blood River* (Broadside Press, 1983), *Rainrituals* (Broadside Press, 1989), and *Shrines* (Third World Press, 2004), and a book of commentary on the political uses of environment in the United States, *Tower and Dungeon: A Study of Place and Power in American Culture*. She is also lead editor of the anthology, *A Different Image: The Legacy of Broadside Press*, selected as a Notable Book of Michigan for 2005 by the Library of Michigan.

Parneshia Jones is a recipient of the Gwendolyn Brooks Poetry Award and the Margaret Walker Short Story Award. She has been published in several anthologies, and has been featured on Chicago Public Radio-Chicago Amplified Series. Jones is a member of the Affrilachian Poets, a collective of Black voices from Appalachia, and has performed her work all over the United States. She holds an MFA from Spalding University in Louisville, Kentucky.

Gaye Theresa Johnson holds a B.A. in Sociology and Ethnic Studies from the University of California at San Diego, and a PhD in American Studies from the University of Minnesota. Her areas of expertise are twentieth century U.S. history; race and racism; social movements and identities, and cultural history with an emphasis on music. Johnson's publications include articles and book reviews in *Aztlán: A Journal of Chicano Studies*, *The Comparative American Studies Journal*, *The Journal of the American Studies Association of Texas*, the *National Women's Studies Association Journal*, and two edited collections on race and popular culture. In 2006, her essay, "'Sobre Las Olas': A Mexican Genesis in Borderlands Jazz" won Best Paper in Comparative Ethnic Studies from the American Studies Association. She spent the 2008-2009 academic year at Stanford University in the Center for Comparative Studies in Race and Ethnicity. Johnson is completing a manuscript entitled *The Future Has a Past: Politics, Music and Memory in Afro-Chicano Los Angeles*.

Haki R. Madhubuti is a poet, publisher, editor and educator. He has published 24 books (some under his former name, Don L. Lee) and is one of the world's best-selling authors of poetry and non-fiction. He has facilitated workshops and served as guest/keynote speaker at colleges, universities, libraries and community centers in the U.S. and abroad. Madhubuti is the founder of Third World Press, and co-founder of the Institute of Positive Education/New Concept School and the Betty Shabazz International Charter School in Chicago, Illinois. In 2010, he joined the faculty of Depaul University.

Nathan McCall has served as a reporter for newspapers such as *The Washington Post*, where he worked until taking a leave of absence to write his best selling memoir, *Makes Me Wanna Holler, A Young Black Man in America*. McCall's second publication, released in 1997, is a series of personal essays titled, *What's Going On*. In 2007, he made his fiction debut with *Them* (Atria Books), cited by *Publishers Weekly* as one of the best books of 2007, and reached No. 1 on the *Essence* magazine bestseller list and was nominated for the 2008 Townsend Prize for Fiction. In addition to writing, McCall works as a visiting lecturer in the African American Studies Department at Emory University in Atlanta. www.nathanmccall.net

Tony Medina was born and raised in New York City. He has published thirteen books and his poetry, essays and fiction appear in over eighty anthologies and publications. His most recent works include *I and I, Bob Marley* and *My Old Man Was Always on the Lam*. Associate Professor of Creative Writing at Howard University, Medina earned a MA and PhD from Binghamton University, SUNY. tmedina@howard.edu

E. Ethelbert Miller is the board chair of the Institute for Policy Studies and the director of the African American Resource Center at Howard University. His most recent book is a second memoir, *The 5th Inning*. Mr. Miller is often heard on National Public Radio. www.eethelbertmiller.com

Indigo Moor is a poet, author, and playwright living in Rancho Cordova, CA. His second book *Through the Stonecutter's Window* was selected for the

2009 Cave Canem Northwestern University Poetry Prize. His first book *Tap-Root* was published in 2007 as part of Main Street Rag's Editor's Select Poetry Series. He is a 2003 recipient of Cave Canem's writing fellowship in poetry, former vice president of the Sacramento Poetry Center, and an editor for the *Tule Review*. He is the winner of the 2005 Vesle Fenstermaker Poetry Prize for Emerging Writers and the 2008 Jack Kerouac Poetry Prize. www.indigomoor.com

jessica Care moore was called "one of the most important voices of her generation" by *Essence Magazine*. She is the author of *The Words Don't Fit in My Mouth, The Alphabet Verses The Ghetto* and *God is Not an American*. She is also the CEO of Moore Black Press. A Detroit native, moore has read her work in South Africa, Europe and all over the US. She is well known for her historical win on "It's Showtime At The Apollo" and is an Apollo Legend. www.mooreblackpress.com and www.jessicacaremoore.net

Opal Moore is the author of the poetry collection, *Lot's Daughters*. Her poetry, fiction and essays have appeared in journals and anthologies, including *Shaping Memories: Reflections of African American Women Writers, The Notre Dame Review, nocturnes: a (re)view of the literary arts,* and *Honey, Hush: An Anthology of African American Women's Humor*. Moore teaches creative writing at Spelman College in Atlanta, GA.

Eugene B. Redmond is a poet, critic, editor, publisher, educator and activist who has been an influential figure in African American literature since the 1960s Black Arts Movement. He is the recipient of numerous awards and is the Poet Laureate of East St. Louis. He is author of the seminal work, *Drumvoices*, and founder and editor of the literary journal *Drumvoices Revue*.

Sonia Sanchez, author of over twenty-five poetry collections, plays, and children's books. She has lectured at more than five hundred universities and colleges in the United States and had traveled extensively. She was the first Presidential Fellow at Temple University, where she began teaching in 1977, and held the Laura Carnell Chair in English there until her retirement in 1999. Sanchez has received the Community Service Award from the National Black Caucus of State Legislators, the Outstanding Arts Award from the Pennsylvania Coalition of 100 Black Women, the Peace and Freedom Award from Women International League for Peace and Freedom (WILPF), the Pennsylvania Governor's Award for Excellence in the Humanities, a National Endowment for the Arts Award, and a Pew Fellowship in the Arts. She lives in Philadephia.

Michael Simanga is an activist, multi-discipline artist. He is author of the novel *In the Shadow of the Son*, poetry, short fiction and essays. His latest work is a historical study of the Congress of African People. www.michaelsimanga.com

Renee Simms is a poet and writer originally from Detroit, MI. A graduate of the University of Michigan and Wayne State University Law School, she received her MFA in Creative Writing from Arizona State University. Her work appears in the anthologies *Voices from Leimert Park* (Tsehai 2006), *Mischief Caprice & Other Poetic Strategies* (Red Hen Press 2004), and *Step into a World: A Global Anthology of the New Black Literature* (Wiley & Sons 2000). Her poems and stories may also be found in *North American Review, African Voices*, *Hawai'i Review, Inkwelll, Our Stories, Oregon Literary Review*, and *42 Opus*. A Cave Canem and PEN Emerging Voices Fellow, she currently lives and teaches in Arizona.

Patricia Smith is a 2008 National Book Award Finalist for her collection of poetry *Blood Dazzler*. Her poems have appeared in various publications and anthologies including *Poetry*, *The Paris Review*, *The Spoken Word Revolution*, and *The Oxford Anthology of African-American Poetry*. She is an instructor of poetry, performance, and creative writing. www.wordwoman.ws

Edward S. Spriggs has had poetry published in several anthologies and small publications dating from 1965. He was an editor of the *Journal of Black Poetry* and an editor and publisher of *Black Dialogue Magazine*. He produced poetry readings and was a filmmaker before becoming the first permanent director of the Studio Museum in Harlem. He is the founding director and curator emeritus of Hammonds House Museum in Atlanta from which he retired in 2002. Since retirement, he continues as an art curator, essayist, lecturer, and poet based in Atlanta.

Sharan Strange grew up in Orangeburg, SC, was educated at Harvard College, and received an MFA in poetry from Sarah Lawrence College. She is the author of *Ash* (Beacon Press, 2001), winner of the 2000 Barnard New Women Poets Prize, selected by Sonia Sanchez. Her work has been published in various publications and anthologies. She is a professor of English at Spelman College in Atlanta, GA.

Askia M. Toure' epic poet, visionary, Africana Studies pioneer, is a co-founder of the historic Black Arts Movement. He is author of eight books, including national award-winning *From the Pyramids to the Projects*, and *Dawn-Song*. His film, *Double-Dutch a Gathering of Women*, was a prize-winner at the 2003 Roxbury Film Festival. He resides in Boston and is a master-artist-in-residence at Northeastern University. Askia38@yahoo.com.

Natasha Trethewey earned an M.A. in poetry from Hollins University and an M.F.A. in poetry from the University of Massachusetts. Her first collection of poetry, *Domestic Work* (2000), was the Cave Canem Poetry Fellow Prize for the best first book by an African American poet. *Bellocq's Ophelia* (2002) was her second collection, and her third, *Native Guard* (Houghton Mifflin, 2006), received the Pulitzer Prize for Poetry. Trethewey's honors include the Bunting Fellowship from the Radcliffe Institute for Advanced Study at Harvard and fellowships from the National Endowment for the Arts, the Guggenheim Foundation, and the Rockefeller Foundation. She is professor of English at Emory University where she holds the Phillis Wheatley Distinguished Chair in Poetry.

Quincy Troupe is the author of seventeen books, including eight volumes of poetry, the latest of which is *The Architecture of Language*, recipient of the 2007 Paterson Award for Sustained Literary Achievement. He received the 2003 Milt Kessler Poetry Award for *Transcircularities: New and selected Poems* (Coffee House Press, 2002), selected by *Publishers Weekly* as one of the ten best books of poetry published in 2002. He is Professor Emeritus of Creative Writing and American and Caribbean Literature at the University of California, San Diego, was the first official Poet Laureate of the State of California and is currently editor of *Black Renaissance Noire,* an academic, cultural, political and literary journal published by the Institute of African American Affairs at New York University. He lives in Harlem, NY.

Sala Udin stood mesmerized, along with 250,000 others, when as a 20 year old, he witnessed Dr. Martin Luther King, Jr. deliver the "I Have A Dream" speech in August, 1963. A little over a year later, he found himself a Freedom Rider on his way to battle segregation in Mississippi. He rode the wave of "Black Power" as the front lines of the movement shifted from the south to the nation's urban centers. He was a part of the 1970 founding convention of the Congress of African People and chaired the Pittsburgh Chapter. After 25 years of organizing, Sala Udin was elected to the Pittsburgh City Council, where he served for 11 years. He responded early to the prospect of a presidential run by Senator Barack Obama and formed African Americans For Obama in Pittsburgh. On January 20, 2009, Sala again found himself on the Washington mall to witness the swearing in of the first African American President of the Unites States, 46 years after Dr. King sparked a dream in the nation. www.salaudin.com.

Frank X Walker a native of Danville, KY, is a graduate of the University of Kentucky, and completed an MFA in Writing at Spalding University. He is a founding member of the Affrilachian Poets, the editor of *America! What's My Name? The "Other" Poets Unfurl the Flag* (Wind Publications, 2007), and *Eclipsing a Nappy New Millennium.* He is also the author of four poetry collections, *When Winter Come: The Ascension of York* (University Press of Kentucky, 2008), *Buffalo Dance: The Journey of York* (University Press of Kentucky, 2003), winner of the 35th Annual Lillian Smith Book Award; and *Affrilachia* (Old Cove Press, 2000), a Kentucky Public Librarians' Choice Award nominee. He currently serves as associate professor in the Department of English at the University of Kentucky, and is the proud editor and publisher of *PLUCK!, The New Journal of Affrilachian Art & Culture.*

Nagueyalti Warren is a Cave Canem Poetry Fellow, poet, editor, and professor at Emory University. She is author of *Margaret,* winner of the Naomi Long Madgett Poetry Prize, and editor of *Temba Tupu! (Walking Naked) Africana Women's Poetic Self-Portrait.* Her poems have appeared in *Essence Magazine, PLUCK! The Journal of Affrilachian Arts & Culture,* and *The Courtland Review.* www.nagueyalti.com.

Shawn L. Williams is a writer living in Stone Mountain, GA. He is an associate professor of Humanities at Georgia Perimeter College and author of the book *I'm a Bad Man: African American Vernacular Culture and the Making of Muhammad Ali* (Lulu Press).

Demetrice Anntía Worley is an associate professor of English at Bradley University. Her debut poetry collection is *Tongues in My Mouth* (Main Street Rag 2011). In addition, she is the co-editor of *Language and Image in the Reading-Writing Classroom* (LEA 2002) and *African American Literature* (McGraw-Hill 1998); and co-compiled *Reflections on a Gift of Watermelon Pickle and Other Modern Verse* (ScottsForesman 1995). Her poetry has appeared in anthologies and journals. Her honors include Third Prize, Split This Rock 2009 Poetry Contest; Semi-finalist (2006 and 2009), Crab Orchard Press First Book Contest; and Finalist, *Spoon River Poetry Review*, 2002 Editor's Prize. Also, she is a Cave Canem Poetry Fellow. She holds a D.A. in English from Illinois State University and an M.A. in English from University of Illinois, Urbana.